Crete 1941

PRAISE FOR
Crete 1941

Crete 1941 is both a compelling tribute to heroism under threat and a subtle study of the epic and its place in the modern world. By attending to the history of political poetry in such a compelling and informed way, Dr Cadogan proves that poetry can still contend with the most difficult questions about bravery, belief, and allegiance at a time of war, and that it can serve the memory of those who deserve the highest respect.

- **Dr Dan Sperrin**, University of Oxford, Faculty of English

Reclaiming the skill, force and wisdom of millennia of European and South Pacific poetic taonga, and acknowledging the complexities of heroic deeds, error, and crime, Crete 1941 is no less than a commemoration and analysis of the human condition *in extremis*. In post-heroic times, this is a most difficult task and Crete 1941 tackles it with sensitivity, wit and bravura.

- **Dr Norman Franke**, Conjoint Research Fellow, University of Newcastle, Australia

Like the epics of old, Crete 1941 is the story of the deeds of men and women that are worthy of recording and retelling. The battle of Crete may have ended in the defeat of the allied forces, but the bravery of the defenders of the island is still celebrated in Greece as one of the most heroic moments of that war. Crete 1941 offers a new perspective to this event: that of the New Zealand allied forces to whom the island was an alien world, providing insight and understanding of the experience of fighting on the other side of the world. Crete 1941 is more than a historical epic. It is a guide to knowledge: knowledge of the mythical and historical past, but also knowledge of the self, collective and personal.

- **Dr Olympia Bobou**, School of Culture and Society, Aarhus University

Bernard takes a unique approach to describing the emotions, the sounds, the players and the stage of the Battle of Crete within a poetic saga. He captures the clash and collision of our Treaty cultures within this tale of tragedy. I hope that our future generations will study Bernard's poetic work for its insight into the political forces at play and how this piece of history has played its part in our national identity.

  – **Tania Te Rangingangana Simpson**,
    author, The Last Maopo, Member, Waitangi Tribunal

Of all the military campaigns fought in Greece during the second world war, the Battle of Crete is remembered as one of the strongest acts of defiance against Nazi aggressors. During ten days of fighting, 274 Australians and 671 New Zealanders were killed, and more than 3000 captured. Cretan villagers risked their lives hiding many ANZAC troops on the island, forging special bonds among the nations of Greece, Australia and New Zealand. Eighty years on, Crete 1941 brings all this to life, highlighting the sacrifices of our forebears so we may lead a peaceful, liberated life. This book is a sensitive account which deserves all the accolades and respect it will doubtless receive.

  – **Tony Tsourdalakis**, President,
    Cretan Federation of Australia & New Zealand

CRETE 1941

Crete 1941

Bernard Cadogan

TUWHIRI

Wellington
Aotearoa New Zealand

CRETE 1941

First published 2021

The Tuwhiri Project

PO Box 6626, Wellington 6141

Aotearoa New Zealand

www.tuwhiri.nz

© 2021 Bernard Cadogan

This book is copyright. Apart from fair dealing for the purpose of private study, research, or review, as permitted under the Copyright Act, no part may be reproduced by any process without prior permission from the publishers.

ISBN 978-0-473-58788-8 (Paperback Aotearoa New Zealand)

ISBN 978-0-473-58789-5 (Paperback print-on-demand)

ISBN 978-0-473-58790-1 (ePub)

ISBN 978-0-473-58791-8 (Kindle)

ISBN 978-0-473-58792-4 (PDF)

A catalogue record for this book is available from the National Library of New Zealand

Kei te pātengi raraunga o Te Puna Mātauranga o Aotearoa te whakarārangi o tēnei pukapuka

Edited by Ramsey Margolis and Winton Higgins

Cover design: minimum graphics

Cover photo: New Zealand soldiers in an olive grove on Crete. Bill Spence (front left), Billy Moran (front right). Rowe EKS. DA-11032. Alexander Turnbull Library.

Book design: John Houston

Set in Signifier, National 2 and Feijoa Display by Klim Type Foundry, Wellington, Aotearoa New Zealand

10 9 8 7 6 5 4 3 2 1

In memoriam Konstantinos Stephanopoulos *(1926–2016),*
President of Greece 1995–2005

CRETE 1941

Contents

Karakia by Trevor J Moeke	xi
Foreword by Rt Hon Trevor Mallard	xiii
Introduction	1
Sonnet for Lieutenant Ngaurimu VC	3
Crete 1941	
Canto 1	5
Canto 2	33
Canto 3	57
Canto 4	81
Canto 5	107
Sonnet to Hölderlin	131
Coda	133
About the author	137
Thanks	138
Tuwhiri thanks	139
About Tuwhiri	140

CRETE 1941

Karakia

A dedication to the 28th Māori Battalion, and to this book *Crete 1941*, its skilled pen, its articulate rendering, recanting uniquely of and for their feats. Invocation launching acknowledgement and prayer, drawn from the Battalion's own 1941 open air desert 'recording' to send 'home'. Remastered also from writings, poems, insights, stories and songs of their feats and families.

> Hear now as hearts beat in unison, see the ancestral Matariki (Pleiades) constellation.
> The new year, time to close, to surrender, to farewell – renew, refresh, and to set forth, anew.
> Celebrate and honour.
> As they did. As we must. As always!
> So then, vigilance, a prayer of dedication:
>
> 'Kia hiwa rā! Kia hiwa rā!'
> 'Te kokoma i te kōkōmako
> Ko te hautapu e rite ki te kai nā Matariki
> Tapa reireia koia tapa
> Tapa kononua koiana tukua
> Hei auē. Hei!!!'
> 'Ka maumahara mātou ki a rātou.'
>
> Hark! In mem'ry lingering – all too stoic here then tempered fired furnaced face of death
> Aloft now you brave ones – as galaxied ancestral markers to the

CRETE 1941

heavens – harbinger stars to your oceans' voyagers' navigators yielding life's sacred renewal
Hear then the dawned heliacal rise of Matariki – the constellation's altars heralded – invoke them here – season renewed!
We hold them.
We hold them.
We hold them, those brave ones...
'We will remember them.'
'...... Ah Mem'ry lingering!'

Na

Trevor J Moeke
Ngati Porou, Ngati Awa, Ngati Kahungunu
Wellington, NZ
August 2021

Foreword

By Rt Hon Trevor Mallard

The stories of Maui, Kupe, Cook, Waitangi, Ruapekapeka, Parihaka, Maungapōhatu, Gallipoli and Michael Joseph Savage have helped shape our understanding of ourselves as New Zealanders. 'Crete 1941', Bernard Cadogan's epic poem culminates with the entry of the 28th (Māori) Battalion into the battle and in doing so brings together warriors over the millennia so different and yet with so much in common.

'Crete 1941' is written in Spenserian stanzas, made famous by the 16th century allegorical epic 'The Faerie Queene' which celebrated the Tudor dynasty and especially Elizabeth I. To be able to tell a story of such length within the discipline of the eight lines of iambic pentameter followed by the single twelve syllable iambic line per stanza is something no one other than Cadogan is currently capable of doing. It has a beat, a rhythm, which I most enjoyed while reading it aloud.

Bernard Cadogan is a New Zealander who in recent decades has lived near Oxford in the UK. He is a thinker who applies his considerable intellect to issues of both our past and our future. Cadogan's work on Sir George Grey provides considerable insight into how and why the British imperialist approach changed, and therefore the colonisation of Aotearoa differed so much from South Africa and Australia. His advice to me, and to other Ministers, in developing a strategy to counter the Don Brash-led attack on equity in Aotearoa in 2004 and 2005 was invaluable.

As is clear early in 'Crete 1941', Bernard Cadogan has an extensive understanding of Greek and Roman gods. Like Arapeta Awatere, later Commanding Officer of 28th (Māori) Battalion did when exhorting his men, he uses Greek and Latin as well as English proverbs and poetry to emphasise his meaning. He weaves together the lessons of ancient places and battles with the fight for Crete.

Unlike many from modern Aotearoa I've been lucky, through sheer coincidence, to have had contact with Cretans and some extensive discussions about our role in their battle. An early Petone Labour Party Hall, built in the time of Harry Holland and now the home of the Lighthouse Cinema, for many years housed the Wellington Cretan Club. We used it for election day and night activities under their ownership.

A highlight of lockdown and the later part of 2020 for me was the arrival nearly every day of a few more stanzas of what was to become 'Crete 1941'. It wasn't always easy to get my head around. Google generally helped, the notes for each Canto in this edition certainly do.

'Crete 1941' has added two items to my bucket list. First to read this epic on Hikurangi, the maunga that inspired so many men of the 28th (Māori) Battalion, and secondly to read it again high in the Asterouia or Psilortis mountains. Both experiences can only help educate me.

Trevor Mallard
Wainuiomata 2021

Introduction

Between 20 May and 1 June 1941, New Zealand experienced its Dunkirk moment as Allied forces under Major General Bernard Freyberg resisted the German invasion of Crete, before retreating across the Libyan Sea to Egypt. For Greek forces, this battle marked their final resistance on Greek territory before continuing the fight from exile. The war became a partisan war in occupied Greece that became the prelude to the Greek civil war of 1946–49. For Māori, the Battle of Crete was the first time Māori soldiers, in the form of the 28th (Māori) Battalion, entered the theatre of war between the nations as a fighting infantry force, and not as military pioneers, as sappers, diggers and trench-builders.

Māori and Pākeha New Zealanders found themselves fighting for the oldest site of European civilisation – of the literate palace-based Minoan civilisation that began over 4000 years ago. That this was the case can only be understood now. No one in 1941 had the time to reflect on this background. The island has borne a reputation for both a golden age and appalling cruelty. Virgil and Dante explored this profound ambivalence of both Crete and European civilisation in their own ways.

An epic poem seemed a good way to capture the significance of our failed defence of Crete for both ourselves and the Greeks of Crete. The New Italian Epic (NIE) of the cryptic Italian writing syndicate Wu Ming hinted at how this might be done. I decided to revisit the court epics of Ferrara, the colonial epics in similar form by Edmund Spenser and Alfred Domett, one-time Premier of New Zealand: 'The Faerie Queene' and 'Ranolf and Amohia'.

Other southern-hemisphere nations have national epics. At 2475 lines, *Crete 1941* is about as long as Argentina's gaucho epic by José Hernández,

El Gaucho Martín Fierro. Chile has the three book epic *La Araucana*, by Alonso de Ercilla. South Africa has Mazisi Kunene's *Emperor Shaka the Great*; while Australia has Rex Ingamells's *The Great South Land*. Composed in West Oxford during the first UK pandemic lockdown of 2020, and edited in the Upper Cherwell Valley at Woodford Halse in 2021 during the third lockdown, 'Crete 1941' is an attempt to give New Zealand an inclusive national poem.

Credit should be given to the form used in this epic – the Spenserian stanza. Such a form creates its own momentum; the question is, what does it do? After a trial run of the first 15 stanzas of Canto I, I realised that the form would deliver tragedy, atrocity, reflection, humour, irony and geniality without any bathos or confusion. Homer's wine-dark sea sparkles in the sunlight!

'Crete 1941' ponders how two historically colonised peoples – indigenous New Zealand Māori and Cretans – responded to Nazi aggression. It's a reflection on the virtue of small countries, on great power aggression, and on the necessity for an international order to resist racism and provide alternatives to the brute exercise of sheer force.

The Latin Epicurean epic and poetics of Lucretius, Virgil and Horace influenced this work, and a personal conversation with President Stephanopoulos of Greece inspired this poem. It is also an attempt to offer a prelude to the centennial year of Hone Tuwhare's birth as well as to commemorate the 80th anniversary of the Battle of Crete and the 200th anniversary of the commencement of the Greek War of Independence at Sfakia, Crete.

It is with immense pleasure that I acknowledge the secular-Buddhist counterpart to Graeco-Roman Epicureanism, and express my heartfelt thanks to The Tuwhiri Project for such exceptionally sensitive and careful editing and presentation of the poem and its notes. I never had to explain anything. New Zealand has lacked a publisher unafraid of ideas and intelligence, and Tuwhiri has now closed that gap.

Bernard Cadogan

Blackwell's Bookshop, Oxford, UK

17 May 2021

Sonnet for Lieutenant Ngārimu VC

If you want to know me, know my star
and know my mountain. I am the firstborn,
Atutahi, and first light from afar,
Hikurangi. My people at dawn
look on that star as a mountain in space,
which I saw low down the other evening
in Africa. Canopus is a place
where we have laid aside fear and grieving.
First the stars are made out as tiny sparks,
then come the meteors fired like tracers.
Over the mountain that was our ark,
Atutahi stands aside and faces
up to solitude night after night.
I hold Hill 209 – my last fight.

Te Kaha
Bay of Plenty
5 November 2019

Lieutenant Te Moananui-a-Kiwa Ngārimu VC (1918–43) was awarded a posthumous Victoria Cross for a conspicuous feat of arms in Tunisia, just short of his 25th birthday. He died on 27 March 1943, after serving in Greece, on Crete, in Egypt and Libya. He had been chosen for intelligence duties in England.

Ngārimu came from the Ngāti Porou iwi of the East Cape of New Zealand, whose sacred mountain is Mt Hikurangi, which does indeed receive the dawn first in summer of any mainland or country.

Atutahi is Canopus, a most holy star, prominent in the southern hemisphere, but appearing in the northern hemisphere only in winter south of 37ºN. In Māori legend, Atutahi 'the firstborn' stands apart from the Milky Way, and refuses to join those stars, in defiance of Rangi the Sky Father.

Crete 1941

Canto I

1

    Crete is the island. No one is called
    to it save Cretans, who live on the ridge
    with Africa beyond. There time is stalled,
    but starts up again to circuit a bridge
    going nowhere east-west. Place where damage
    has left a golden age half-flowering,
    half-petrified, because self-abridged
    on a heading due north and towering
    like a wave, rearing up and yet underpowered,

2

    likely to collapse and dissolve mid-sea
    despite the height of Spring's sublime snow.
    Generals fall back on Crete, not to harry
    the mainland or strike back in one go,
    but clutch onto freight, as supercargoes
    on a failing ship with materiel
    of war in the hold. Once there, we just know
    our exile from Hellas is perpetual,
    unless we surrender the mere ethereal

3

and accept the violence of our failure.
We have to go back by another way.
The Minotaur is a bloody jailer
whose occupation is to darken day
whether in the Bronze Age, now, or May
1941, with shadow-races
which course the slopes. But death is what stays
in the sun, as fast labyrinths chase
after people on the run, then veer into space.

4

On Everest 'we knocked the bugger off' –
quipped the Kiwi Good Keen Man. Not on Crete
where we left the Greeks in long low troughs
the beast fed from. They lived our defeat
three years long, while we went on to repeat
hard success, once we learned to dance the maze
of violence. Daedalus built the high seat
and dancing ground where Minos phases
in with Rhadamanthus, judging by the traces

4 – Sir Edmund Hillary (1919-2008) who climbed Mt Everest in 1953 made the comment in l.1. Barry Crump (1935-96) a New Zealand author and outdoors devised that limiting form of masculinity of 'the good keen man'.

CANTO I

5

    we leave for them on the shifting floor.
    The inhabitants of Crete come first,
    not nation-building stories which ignore
    the true condition of myth as it bursts
    on the mind. The Minotaur is a worst
    case scenario, a monstrous creature
    known only to high opera and verse,
    enfilading air, landing on beaches.
    A persona of recognisable features

6

    which on that occasion was German.
    Ezekiel's beasts tread out their station.
    Those holy chimaeras are each sermons
    against the tyrannical nation
    which sets itself in abomination
    and comes wearing the Minotaur mask,
    to impose tribute and occupation.
    But who are the Cretans, we ought to ask.
    Who were the Eteo-Cretans? That strange ballast

7

    on the manifest and bill of lading
    which Odysseus gave Penelope
    of the isle, by degrees invading
    his own palace in the panoply
    of that beast – a tramp. Hospitality
    alone protected him in the household.
    It is only under the canopy
    of cultures of welcome that we are told
    how we live in the world, find ourselves enfolded.

8

Forget Homer – Cretans are the people
of the *Erotokritos* – epic – courts
could not produce. Instead, upheaval
fashioned people whose poet exhorted
them to resilience and the resort
to love. Gyges' Ring, true love's blind test,
the Hellenistic novel were wrought
out of Frankish romance into a crest
like that of Mount Ida, into a floating chest

9

like the one Perseus and his mother
emerged from, for the hero to turn
the Gorgon to stone, then discover
Andromeda. The Old Man of Crete yearns
for one river, not just Lethe which churns
in the Underworld for Arethousa.
Do not ask where that spring rises, to spurn
darkness. Ask who she is and you lose her.
Geopolitics is the wreck of Medusa.

---

8 - The legend of the Ring of Gyges can be sourced at Plato's *Republic* 2. 359a.

9 - Arethousa is the heroine of the much-loved 17th century Greek epic, *Erotokritos* by Vitzentzos Kornaros (1558–1613/14) of Candia in Crete. She is named after the fountain Arethousa, the water of which was supposed to flow undersea from Arcadia to Syracuse. The Old Man of Crete is found in Dante's *Inferno* XIV 28.

10

    What happened on the island? What happened
when – if at all? Palace leads to palace,
the double axe, the bright throne room weaponed
with griffons. The anecdotal malice
of sacrifice, prove they were zealous
about Zeus – his nativity and flight
after his siblings fed a jealous
father. Such a meal would have been the plight
of Knossos, if youngsters were taken out of sight

11

    for Asterion to rend evil
from evil. We might want to believe
Europe always to have been longeval
for palatial terror, since the received
wisdom holds that this Atlantis cleaved
theophagy unto tauroctony.
After which such severe justice breathed
forth a golden age's monotony,
labrys and sickle joined in orchidectomy.

---

11 – Asterion is the Minotaur's name. Read Jorge Luis Borges' 'The House of Asterion', and also Dante's *Inferno* XIV 27 where he talks about Crete.

CRETE 1941

12

'We did it for civilization,'
said Big Bill Massey in a small calm voice
at Versailles, his one contribution
to the Grand Siècle. Myth gets foisted
onto fact as if decisionist choice
requires a lineage back to torment
and to Minos, so we might rejoice
that our state shows signs of improvement,
finds indemnity through the art of government.

13

Virgil and Dante need the labyrinth
to be true – none can read them otherwise.
They need to fell the bloody terebinth
underneath the stars, expose the guises
of bull-men and Pasiphaë, surprise
us with their gospels of murdered heifers,
sacrificial steers and a cloud of flies,
leading to citizen bees and zephyrs
of accord, which put the State back into cypher.

12 – William Massey, prime minister of New Zealand 1912–25.
13 – I refer to that truly great poem, *Georgics IV* of Publius Vergilius Maro, and to Dante's *Inferno* XII 11 and XIV 27.

14
　The labrys cuts both ways. When we kill
the victim, we do something to ourselves.
So we watch ourselves sever, and spill
just the same. This happens when we delve
into time that is not our own, and shelve
where we properly belong a moment.
We look at our wound and find no salve
for it. Then we know poison will ferment
and it is of no consequence if we repent.

15
　'You can't kick against geography!'
argued Venizelos the ethnarch,
who had to live in aetiology.
He was a man of daring wiles who harked
back to myth – more Theseus than Bismarck
for Greece. Minos at war with Minotaur
as he fought the palace and its claque.
Deafened by gold cicadas of the law,
in his youth he was once Crete's Juarez or Cavour.

---

14 - The Cretan patriot Eleftherios Venizelos (1864–1936) was prime minister of Greece 1910–15, 1915, 1917–20, 1924, 1928–32, 1932 and 1933. He had previously held portfolios in the Cretan state 1899–1910. Benito Juarez (1810–72) was president of Mexico 1858–72, while Camillo Benso, count of Cavour (1806–61) was prime minister of Sardinia 1852–59, 1860–61 and the first prime minister of Italy in 1861.

16

Enosis necessitated schism –
such was his insight, that only rupture
like the Old Man of Crete's, seeped the chrism
of blood. It would take social fracture
and streams of atrament to recapture
all of Greece. It would need paidophagy
of its own. Venizelos in rapture
is trialing wireless telegraphy
from the front – you can't kick against demography.

17

The monster came to in the labyrinth
of nations, wondered where the goddesses
had gone, why the snake-ladies left their plinths.
He comprehended at last the oddest
nightmare he had gone through, how immodest
he had been to imitate Pocock's
centaur, and vault through time in protest.
He woke up a bull right down to the hocks.
All he could do was feed on party girls and jocks.

---

16 – Cronos ate all his divine children except for Zeus, whom his mother hid in a cave under Mt Ida.

17 – John Greville Agard Pocock MNZM (b. 1924) is the great New Zealand historian of political thought at Johns Hopkins University, who represented President Andrew Jackson as a centaur in his *The Machiavellian moment: Florentine political thought and the Atlantic republican tradition* (Princeton University Press, 1975).

18

    Goddesses are honorary women.
    Government has queenship inherent
    whether women wear cloches or denim.
    Crete is a land of estranged parents
    and butchered gods. The local adherents
    and newcomers attempted matchmaking
    with results that were hardly coherent.
    This pantheon of standoffs and faking
    led to Phoenician princesses for the taking,

19

    and those strange origins of Europe
    involving bulls and a woman from Tyre.
    Zeus brought up on wild honey syrup,
    on tej in a cave, buckthorn slow to fire
    to bitter the mead, just as he required.
    Rhamnus is hardly an Aryan name.
    Zeus had a touch of Africa hardwired
    into him. The Middle East too can claim
    this babe on the Cretan massif, nurtured in shame.

---

19 - Rhamnus is a town in Crete, and the botanical name of buckthorn as well. Tej is Ethiopian mead and Communion wine.

20
>Minos made a nine-yearly ascent
to the cave of Zeus – whether Psychro
or the Idaean Cave is not meant
to matter. These are ideal lands Plato
never hiked, nor modern friends with velcro
backpacks, throughout Greece. Minos' purpose
was legislation, which Zeus vetoed
or else reviewed. The 'Laws' three sherpas'
hold their summit along the way, during surplus

21
>dialogue, which even they compare
to a headless monster. Theseus
is the Athenian when the beast rears
into view. The tyrant slain, catharsis
is possible, the text a prosthesis
for a real pilgrimage to the god's birth.
More interesting: the god's anamnesis
when Zeus died. His tomb either a dearth
of sites, or the face of Mt Juktas laid on earth.

20 – I refer to Plato's late-life dialogue, the 'Laws', or 'Nomoi'. Sherpas are officials and diplomats who provide expert advice and support to leaders at international conferences.
21 – Look at a picture of the silhouette of Mt Juktas and see if you can see Zeus' death mask.

22

    Language and place rip apart like velcro.
    The pack flaps about in complicity
    with wind. Crete is no archipelago
    but a land of many ethnicities,
    said Homer. Greek gave it unity
    later. We should listen for a prairie
    of wildflower tongues, in proximity
    to cold mobile Spring and fast-falling tears
    then a gust runs along the ground – and all is clear.

23

    German and English might fit the pack
    but it will not do up. That is not why
    trees shiver with blossom amidst the lack
    of suitable words. We only rely
    on language for other people. The sky,
    warm wind and abundant sun have undone
    the rising land. Poetry is a lie
    that knows the truth, make sure its bag fastens.
    A strange language should contribute a world begun.

---

23 - Homer on Crete in *Odyssey* XIX. 148 ff.

24
'All Cretans are liars,' said the Cretan
Epimenides. The contrary
is not true either – do not be beaten
by how Crete upsets boundaries.
Just one need be true to solve this quandary,
much like at Sodom. Ariadne's orchid
looks like a flower's commentary
on a hawk moth. The rapid bug and torpid
bloom are liars like the labyrinth-lured sphingid.

25
Ariadne the mistress of the dance floor
holds a sacred dance which ties the thread.
She weaves her loom a winding-sheet for war.
It sounds more like sport than a dance, to tread
some game with rules that make the players 'dead'.
Bull-leaping Hemingway and Montherlant
bull-leaping girls too, needed to spread
about the maze, and use their talent
to leap the beast, also as the participants

---

25 – Ariane is French for Ariadne and Thesée is French for Theseus. I refer to Ernest Hemingway (1899–1961) and the French novelist and dramatist Henry de Montherlant (1895–1972).

26

    of a live bull-run in a corral.
    The Gascon *courses landaises* prove what it takes.
    Tauroctony though is done at peril.
    The first court of Europe either faked
    the event and let the boys and girls slake
    their limbs, or somebody did it for real.
    Maybe these games were for the highest stakes
    and sacrificial. Who turned on the deal
    if not Thesée – in a result beyond appeal.

27

    Long after Theseus, Greece, the Germans
    and New Zealand entered this fatal course.
    Crete – a province ruled under firmans,
    until Mehmed V had been forced
    finally by the powers to endorse
    secession a generation before.
    War is an amnesty from remorse.
    Crete's population exchanges tore
    the Turco-Greeks right out – one apple lost its core

---

26 – *Courses landaises* of bull-leaping are really practised as a spectacle sport in Gascony, except they use aggressive cows.

28

Another its peel – the apples eaten
the same. Leyla Saz's music surges
from the kemençe, no longer Cretan.
And what about Karagioules' dirges?
Gone is the Europe that looked to Persia.
We do know what closed eyes are, the lids fast
for good: what a people is like when purged
of sleep. Lots of eyes in closed ranks masked
from sight, the ears removed from being cursed or tasked.

29

To feel for the Turk is to understand
Priam – as Homer did. The Dardanelles
set us against Liman von Sanders
the first of the German generals
we fought. At the Straits he won a signal
triumph for the *West-östlicher Diwan*.
Swept up himself as a war criminal
then discharged, the Great War's dragoman
bore a surname that was once the Jewish Liepmann.

---

28 – Leyla Saz (1850–1936) was a classical Turkish composer and from an Ottoman Greek Muslim family of Cretan origin. Her husband, who was a Turco-Cretan, was Governor of Crete and later prime minister of the Ottoman Empire. Mustafa Karagioules was an exponent of folk song in the Turco-Cretan community. The kemençe is a string instrument from Iran played with a bow.

30

From its ancient resistance to Rome
Germany has had a need for Greece
and believes it a spiritual home.
The Renaissance had never ceased
for the Germans, as they fought to release
energy pent up by Reformation.
That way their spirit could find increase.
For Winckelmann offered the temptation
of shining plaster to the alchemic nation.

31

Those statues were an answer to death.
To have lived intensely and capture
their own ends as if they were seraphs,
to discover themselves through the rapture
of bodily forms, seemed the aperture
for genius through solitary sports
and bespoke mind, to collective stature.
The Germans wanted to be transported
and stay the same – death to be nature unthwarted.

---

30 – Johann Joachim Winckelmann (1717-68) was the German art historian who introduced classical sculpture to *Sturm und Drang* Germany.

32
    Some secret of time is what they glimpsed.
    Gnosis had made existence serious
    for them. The individual was convinced
    he should strive with others at various
    life, and do nothing vicariously.
    Time flowers with the coral of the soul.
    Yet among them many Mariuses,
    as Sulla warned. So busy being whole
    no one regarded the partial man on patrol.

33
    This Nordic fantasy involved the Danes.
    George II (the Second) wore a pair
    of shades and a swagger stick – one who reigned
    in vain. King Aegeus kept staring
    at sails that did not let his eyes appear.
    His kingship's basic tool was a suitcase.
    The right ship would show up with the wrong gear
    when Italy was all there was to face,
    as kings and PMs took turns at being replaced.

33 - George II of Greece (1890-1947) had three reigns - 1922-24, 1935-47, but going into exile from Crete in 1941. He resumed his functions in Athens in 1946. The quip in l.6 paraphrases his own.

34 - Sir Arthur Evans (1851-1941) was the keeper of the Ashmolean Museum at Oxford (1884-1908) and the excavator of Knossos. He commenced work on the site in 1900. He was the last human owner of the Felix Gem which he bequeathed to the Ashmolean. It depicts the scene in Virgil's *Aeneid* when Diomedes inadvertently desecrates the palladium of Troy, which he and

34

Sir Arthur Evans – discoverer
of the palace of Knossos – used to own
the Felix Gem, where Ulysses shudders
at Diomedes' touch. Blood from the prone
guardsman taints the goddess who had not known
our death until then. Hegemony
is only the prophecy postponed:
such is our wretched art's remedy.
The Felix Gem is the Ring of Diomedes.

35

Beware of the shaman and fake marabout
in his burnis. The gem had sad but sage
owners in its keep. Who fouked Denham Fouts?
Not Pope Pius man-slaughtered by his page.
There was the cardinal who played the mage,
the exiled earl, then the colour-blind duke
who liked astronomy, Evans who staged
the Minoan Show – reliant on flukes.
Giving it to the Ashmolean was astute.

Ulysses sought to steal from the Trojans in order to shorten the war. Because of the sacrilege, the Trojan war continued another nine years.

35 – The Felix Gem was owned by Pope Pius II (1458-64), Francesco Cardinal Gonzaga (1444-83), Thomas Howard, 14th earl of Arundel (1586-1646), George Spencer, 4th duke of Marlborough (1739-1817), and Sir Arthur Evans, among others. Denham Fouts (1914-48) was an American socialite from Florida, an original 'Mr Ripley', who became the idol of millionaires, aristocracy, royalty and of famous writers such as Truman Capote.

36

    Gyges' Ring would not have promoted
    such an inconsequential line of men.
    Adolf Hitler came in on remote.
    Time to learn to use Bofors gun and STEN.
    Time to fight in the Aegean again.
    Do not credit him as the Widerchrist.
    He dug the labyrinth wider and penned
    us in. The story is how we missed
    Minotaur, how Germans brought myth to terminus.

37

    New Zealand is Magna Creta. Islands
    there have volcanoes, the mountains have blades
    to divide the rain, part the violence
    of gales and cut to the abyssal shade
    of ocean troughs. *Pounamu* is our jade
    the colour of time. We have minotaurs
    as well – unpenned within palisades
    but a diminished species, adored
    like golden calves, who venally trample and gore.

---

36 – Stefan George (1868–1933) composed his Anti-Christ poem, '*Der Widerchrist*' in 1907.

37 – *Pounamu* is New Zealand nephrite. The ancient jade of China was also nephrite, not jadeite.

38
 Would we wish Minos to recognise
 ours as perfect government – be blessed
 with laws that Magnesia devised?
 For our utopias we should suggest
 Crete as our source of constant regress.
 Our prime minister then – Peter Fraser
 a wise and steady Scot would be our best.
 A country of workers and graziers
 had found the right guide, through the maze of war's brazier.

39
 Bernard Freyberg was a fortunate
 Diomedes. The Palladium cost
 him the war to start with – yet consummate
 soldiering won back the time he had lost –
 showed backstabbing brigadiers who was boss.
 He learned how one tips a Pareto front
 by small margins, made sure he could cross
 the lines. Retreat in depth taught him to shunt
 armies in turn, once he had learned to bear their brunt.

---

38 – Peter Fraser was the Labour Party prime minister of New Zealand 1940–49.

40

General Papagos knew how to hang
onto mountains. He left Thrace where Persians
had once run out of their parasangs
and blocked the Italian incursions.
He thought of mountains the way a surgeon
operates, except he used their bodies
as a shield, the ridges for insertion
of a fast-moving topology
mountain after mountain, and a necrology

41

that did the nation honour. Freyberg learned
times's treacherous behaviour from swimming
the sea's currents, just as gulls and terns
fly Wellington winds. Anywhere brimming
fire and water, the Salamander skimmed,
and set to measure. Straight in meanders
he gave thorough support to a winning
generalissimo. The New Zealander
as capable subaltern – not just Leander.

41 – Lieutenant General Bernard Freyberg VC, 1st Baron Freyberg (1889–1963) was Commander of the 2nd New Zealand Expeditionary Force in the Second World War and Governor-General of New Zealand 1946–52.

42

    The mazes are also in the mountains
of Pindus, where armies fought for catchments,
set up encampments, sessile like plantains,
sending out decimated detachments,
to capture trig stations and gradients
suitable for war. Their no man's lands
were the river flats. Tidy hatchments
of box barrages – 100,000
rounds in 3 miles could not drive them from their grandstands.

43

    The green Aoos, or Vjöse, flowed
in Spring spate beneath battle on the loud
summits, through country of mud, cold and snow.
The Cretan 5th Division are proud
of their bull-leaping, of how such a crowd
of their dead carried the enemy lines
on Mt Trebeshina, held to its shroud
of snow, after war on the anticline
cut them off from their own peaks of Plattenkalk lime.

---

42 – By plantains, I do not mean bananas, but the low-lying northern temperate climate plant

44
> But those Cretans would not get back home.
> During vigils that turned into matins,
> Arethousa reaches through night's black loam.
> For her all day long, the house is battened
> with grief. Her men were eaten by Saturn.
> Dark Aphrodite mourns her unshaven
> Adonis. On his blood falls the pattern
> of her tears. Crete is the proper haven
> for red tears – for the dead brought down to the Graben.

45
> Anemones are what grief turns into.
> Red is rare but grows there just the same.
> On Crete they are windows onto virtù:
> the strange lives of men who somehow dodged shame
> recorded on dog-tags, or the bare name
> of honour. Grief bloomed a poisonous weed
> picked and handled with care, to be reclaimed
> in place of those sent as the monster's feed.
> The law of war – a flower that enters no plea.

44 & 45 – Aphrodite is supposed to have created the anemone or windflower from her tears for Adonis. On Crete there are red, though poisonous, anemones growing in the wild.

46

    Who puts who on trial? The chorus is sent
    back down the lane after its query
    and remonstrance. The soldiers have pent
    emotions, their sense of right contrary
    to the villagers' at Kondomari.
    The jury will be taken to be shot.
    How strange – when everyone is wary
    and Germans want to do things by the dot –
    that woman grinning away at the fatal spot.

47

    These are the masks they wore: the younger men
    put their hands to their faces in fear;
    the gerousia out in the open,
    with their gnarled sticks and unquailed eyes, appear
    indignant from their levelled and fixed stares.
    The people are escorted at gun point
    from a crossroads that made do for a square,
    back through the little maze of disjointed
    households and alleys, on this Monday appointed

---

46 – On the orders of General Kurt Student, four truck-loads of III Luftlande-Sturm-Regiment 1 paratroopers arrived at the village of Kondomari on 2 June 1941 to carry out reprisals on selected men in the village, in retaliation for civilian participation in the battle with 21 and 22 New Zealand Infantry Battalions against the Fallschirmjäger landings at Maleme. German records state 23 died. Local inhabitants claim up to 60 were killed. By presidential decree, Kondomari is a 'martyred village'. The Franz-Peter Weixler film of this incident and stills from it leave a distinct impression.

48

for reprisals. Still fresh from their hangars,
the III Luftlande-Sturm-Regiment
feel the grief that is only anger
for their fallen comrades. A fragment
of humanity masks their movements
as if they were making an arrest
or evacuating the male segment
of the population. The menfolk rest
on a bank, doing their utmost not to get stressed.

49

Some are curious about the process.
Others make out they have done this before.
One fair-head tries quietly to protest
but weeps a little, having implored
a folded handkerchief, which he restores
to his pocket. A conspiracy
to avoid panic is shared by the score
or so men. It would be apostasy
to break fellowship in such a contingency.

---

48 – pronounce 'III' as 'Dritte'. The Gerousia were the council of elders of Sparta.

50

    To a grove that streams into a tunnel
    of leaves – they are told to get up and go.
    This place is about to become a funnel
    towards death. Some senior men try to slow
    things down with calm final pleas – but no,
    the smiling troops fire. There is no reply
    as all of these men receive the blow –
    the tall grimacing boy with hands held high
    older men in waistcoats. People manage to die –

51

    people managed a kill. Hawthorn stays
    on the stone walls as new willow gleams
    and the small bursts of smoke fade away.
    The act was done, never to be redeemed.
    The firing squad used Mausers on that green.
    MP40s were deployed as well.
    What survives is worse than dying's dream.
    That is not sleep where broken bodies fell.
    The faces fast turn to contorted masks and swell.

52

    The dark is stark in fact. Death's ministers
    know this. Those include the judge who decides
    on death and applies perimeters,
    where law and rights and custom collide.
    Satisfaction is not provided
    in all cases. Law does not gather
    an agreement together to elide
    a crime. Judgment is its own endeavour,
    because law knows – 15 seconds is forever.

53
Rather like poetry which is talk
to all or none, without plus and minus.
These stanzas are Ferrara-in-Cork.
Spenser sang colonial detritus
much like New Zealand on the Sinus
Cydonicus after our defeat.
Welcome Rhadamanthus – hello Minos.
Major-General Inglis sat in your seat
to spare General Student a death sentence for Crete.

54
Talos the robot was no help either,
though the Cretans did their best to defend
their homes. Two small atom bombs delivered
world war that constant inconclusive end.
There was no question of making amends –
Greece was the Cold War's first fatality,
as the great powers went on offending.
Socrates said of legality:
law is the discovery of reality.

53 – Cydonia was the ancient name of Chania and Sinus Cydonicus the Roman name for the Kolpos Khanion where the Maleme landings took place. Major General Lindsay Inglis (1894–1966) was the New Zealander who was Chief Judge of the Allied Control Commission Supreme Court. He ensured General Kurt Student (1890–1978) did not receive the death sentence for his invasion and occupation of Crete.

54 – For Talos the robot and the Socrates quote, read the amusing and intriguing Platonic dialogue 'Minos' which may be pseudepigraphical, or may be by Plato or, like some of Shakespeare's plays, a collaborative exercise.

55

    Plato's Clinias, the monitor,
    was to design Crete a perfect polis –
    separate Minos from the Minotaur,
    leaving him the purer part of justice,
    to reign without labyrinth or palace.
    Village elders in their sagacity
    know that Kondomari has this solace –
    where elders say in their capacity
    'Our constitution is the perfect tragedy.'

55 – The character Clinias of Knossos, and the final line, uttered by the elders of Magnesia, feature in Plato's 'Laws'.

CRETE 1941

Canto II

1

    Men who have come from the ends of the earth
    hold the island. They fit into their slot.
    Surprised at the calm and absence of surf,
    they put together Talos the robot,
    as the defender of their new plot
    in the sea. They heard of the Aegean
    from their fathers , but do not know a lot.
    Few had ever visited museums.
    For them Crete has to stand in place of New Zealand.

2

    And they wonder a bit how old-fashioned
    it is, but unless they did sixth form Greek
    in a country where knowledge is rationed,
    it stays a closed book. The range and huge streak
    of snow remind them of home while the peaks
    touch on stars just the same, but left is right
    looking toward the sun, the ground is bleak,
    except where cultivated in tight
    labyrinths of generous leaf and filtered light.

3
    The strangest thing is how they are tonsured
    to the sun, with their hair barbered so close.
    Their manners mix looseness and structure
    although they grin a good deal, their jocose
    humour betrays a glint of the morose,
    at times. They fit in, but lack the words,
    the women, the properties, to suppose
    such a beautiful land would be proffered
    them for good, despite a resemblance which is absurd

4
    to their own. Atlantis is a high wave
    and wall of dream, they will have to pierce
    or surmount. They will either find the cave
    of Zeus, or his tomb. Germans are coerced
    by the same prospect, as they rehearse
    their operation – although they are still
    to see Crete. Neither side knows how fierce
    conflict will get. For now it is all drill,
    as camp life stops any use of personal will.

5
    The Kiwis do not yet know metrics –
    the tierce is the smallest unit of time
    they are able to learn in physics.
    Death could come by milliseconds or climb
    a hospital's plateaux of pain, sublime
    beneath the blue cold. Others will labour
    in agony, until the body declines
    to take more. Who is she – this saviour
    to and from pain, irrespective of behaviour?

6

New Zealand is not at all Greece of course,
despite the likeness their latitudes bring.
Their democracy was like the Norse,
whose weapon-takes and public reasonings
were ordered by law-speakers into *'things'*.
The bare-knuckled brawling thymotic man
under the law's philosopher kings –
criminal and property law's old hands
and schemers against Labour's utopian plans.

7

Bill Stubbs – his mark. Anglo-Saxondom
was the Prussia of the South Pacific's
correlative to Māoridom. Thraldom
in plain words. Prussia was quite specific:
it was still North Sparta. Terrific
proof of the danger of analogies.
Young Ranolf did not get prolific
with Amohia. That apology
for a lad pricked the plain for amphibology.

7 – Bishop William Stubbs (1827–1901) was a regius professor of modern history at Oxford University who promoted essentialist Anglo-Saxonist racial ideology. He was bishop of Chester and then bishop of Oxford. 'Bill Stubbs' is an old joke – see Charles Dickens' *Pickwick papers*.
Alfred Domett (1811–87), premier of New Zealand (1862–63) composed a curious Schopenhauerian epic in Spenserian stanzas, 'Ranolf and Amohia', at the instigation of Governor Sir George Grey. It was about a Scottish laddie and a Māori lass.

8

The god Tūmatauenga grimaces
defiance at Hitler. His face dances
with silent rage. He is a nemesis
no matter what odds – because his stance
is to resist non-being's instances.
Tāwhirimātea, his old foe,
is the one he discerns in the chances
of war and politics. He made fellows
in his image – humankind – to fight that great 'No'.

9

The 28th (Māori) Battalion
are sons of his. Once again, a giant
eagle tries to seize them in its talons.
Whose red maze is it – whose is the patent
minotaur? Either side seems reliant
on the other as the bull – unless one
assumes the beast and lives compliant
with deadly policy. The maze is won
not by who is Theseus – but Asterion.

---

8 – Tūmatauenga, or Tū of the Angry Face is the Māori war god, who created humankind to resist the God of Non-Being and destructive weather, Tāwhirimātea, the eldest sibling of the pantheon, that emerged when Rangi and Papa, the Sky Father and Earth Mother were thrust apart. Tāwhirimātea asserts his father's right against the other children, who insisted on life and being. Compare and contrast with the myth of Zeus and his deposed father, who consumed his offspring.

9 – Until the 17th century, Haast's eagle existed in New Zealand.

10

    Look how many Theseuses there are,
    who took off at dawn in trimotor planes
    and gliders. They look like a seminar
    or Bursenschaft, as they go on campaign.
    This is the day for which they have trained.
    The northern horizon filled with the drone,
    until Crete itself can be made out plain.
    The land approaching – just lying there prone.
    The mountains blinding white stand behind the drop-zone –

11

    more regular than any they have known.
    War's bridegrooms jump out their Tante Ju.
    Some are eager, some have nerves and have thrown
    up a bit, while habit gets quite a few
    out the door. Then each fuselage strews
    its litter in a line. Each piece blossoms
    for when the yellow rising ground rescues
    the suspended man, drifting like flotsam.
    For a moment he is caught to the air's bosom.

---

11 – The Junkers 52 was nicknamed the *Tante Ju* or 'Aunty Ju'.

12

    to those on the ground this is sci fi.
    Technology is often ahead
    of its own game. Icarus in the sky
    simply cannot steer his parachute spread
    towards the ground. He dangled there dead
    in the sights of Enfields. Talos fought back –
    just as he once sunk ships and cremated
    Sardinians. A good many fell slack,
    or doubled up in the harness, struck by attacks

13

    of pain they could not tell from further hits.
    Small showers of their blood land on dry ground.
    The Enlightenment and its eclipse
    produced the most modern youth to be found,
    and some things are seen clearer in dark's bounds.
    Watch Asterion and his sons – the stars.
    How far to fall before death is sounded.
    So few to bound up like jaguars –
    just to lock up the back door to the USSR.

14

    Good Keen Man is about as modern
    as a Matilda tank. No one could doubt
    his courage though, when he had to sojourn
    in battle. Maleme was not a rout
    but a violent scrum which missed out
    on victory, after four day's digest
    of what the next four years would be about.
    Is it right to blame Brigadier Hargest,
    for at last approving Colonel Andrew's request,

15

    To withdraw partly across the runway
    And Hill 107? An aperture.
    Think of the Iliad and those affrays
    when Achaean command was secateured.
    The battle at the ships was a failure
    which occurred at the ditch and palisade
    after Hector led beyond conjecture.
    We lost because we were enfiladed.
    We lost because Germans played rugby past our grade.

16

    In this case Hector won. Braun and Koch
    got out their gliders – one had crash-landed
    on the river bed amid the small rocks
    of the Tavronitis – a bullrush band
    of alluvium like in New Zealand
    except we do not have the cactus.
    Koch to the east knew they would be stranded,
    unless they made for 107's compass
    point perspective above the airfield, and access

---

14 – A 'Matilda' tank was the Infantry Tank Mark II of the British Army from 1936. There were three at Maleme.

15 – *Iliad* XV is where Hector leads the Trojans against the Achaean ships.

16 – I refer to Franz Braun's force which landed west of Maleme and to Walter Koch's which landed east of Maleme below Hill 107. Braun was killed on leaving his glider.

17

    roads to Chania – Freyberg's headquarters.
    To the west Koch watched the palls of smoke grow
    into the sky, heard noise from the slaughter
    of his comrades. Only a constant flow
    of movement would get them to that low
    and comfortable mount, and dislodge
    the New Zealanders. The Greeks following
    the battle with flintlocks clubs and crooks, wedged
    themselves in, and then the German dead were pillaged.

18

    The Germans worked as a divided team.
    Braun was killed and Gericke took over –
    climbing the Tavronitis like a seam.
    Koch – left for dead – was placed under cover.
    Landing east – Meindl took the drover's
    part, shepherding the men towards Hill
    107, and trusting to bravura
    with the operation so close to nihil.
    New Zealand's team discovered no such common will.

18 – Eugen Meindl tactically pulled the situation together for the Fallschirmjäger until he was shot in the chest. If he had not done so, coordinating with Koch's men, the landings at Maleme would have failed as they would at other sites on Crete.

21 – Arthur Rimbaud spoke of the *dérèglement des sens*.

19

Both sides had smashed windscreens from collision.
One from paratroops that did not succeed –
the other did not see war's new vision.
Meindl cleared the glass and proceeded,
till a chest wound left him badly bleeding.
The New Zealanders kept on driving
with the windscreen smashed. Only stealth and speed
had kept some of Koch's unit alive,
until they engaged Andrews' men – having arrived

20

right at the slopes of Hill 107.
The moon and what is left of Greece wane –
Venus after sunset in the heavens –
Merkur at the widest point of its plane,
Mars is the morning, with war in his train,
Jupiter, green Uranus in Taurus –
all of these planets had been detained
by the sun. Saturn though joins with Venus,
while Neptune's wind of ocean tracks Virgo's chorus.

21

So few men step on the summit, surprised.
The planets fast follow the sun west:
the broad ground is now theirs to revise.
Germany is ekstasis at best.
To be even more one's self is the quest,
whereas New Zealand is *dérèglement*
des sens – a constant bungy-jump protest
and fugue, snapped back by their government
by virtue of our umbilical covenant.

22

    The Germans go they know not whither.
    Whether they jump from a height or go down
    a hole, they reach the underworld river
    which is allowed to sweep them on. Some drown
    some will sing blessing some curse their surrounds.
    They are not underwritten. No matter –
    see how good they are at making up ground.
    Survivors come back – perimeters
    are no longer enforced and limits are shattered.

23

    The task is then to reset the norm.
    Bayonets fixed – the slaughtermen-at-arms
    kill the steers late out of barracks and dorms.
    Civilisation is not a charm,
    nor is it the past forever embalmed.
    It is the law reset – and applied
    to oneself. Now in the maze's alarms
    it is hard to tell who is allied
    in such a task – who is really to be decried.

24

    This world where women do not exist,
    is one soldiers flicker in and out of –
    where the pressure of one's sex manifests
    itself in carnage. This hatred is shoved
    with steel, arousing the need for love
    from the body entirely different.
    It is paramount – death is 'she' above
    all else and never 'him' in the events
    of battle – be certain she is the referent.

25

In Chania are women and children –
the polis Freyberg defends and port
of Souda Bay – yet women were seldom,
and now never. The only resorts
were communal. The body is taught
safety nowhere and must tread the maze
of blood and fire throughout these onslaughts
to Maleme and back. Once our moon's phase
is spent, we are embraced to depth beyond men's gaze.

26

The fields are filled with horrible growths
fine young fellows turned to this – a mate
we would have a beer with – makes one loathe.
General Student had chosen not to wait
to send reinforcements. At a huge rate
Gebirgsjäger and light artillery
were landed on the lodgement created
by the New Zealanders' summary
withdrawal, while on the runway ancillary

27

Forces were introduced. Elsewhere – Inglis
at Canea blocked up Prison Alley
where a group of paratroopers lingered,
while Hargest's 5th Division rallied.
Australians under Vesey tallied
up those who had landed at Rethimnon.
Low in munitions – Greek forces sallied
with bayonets outside Heraklion.
On land and sea – air bombardment championed

28

Unternehmen Merkur – lest it falter.
By 22 May our counterattacks
had failed – our offensive was halted.
Fallschirmjäger had got in a crack
behind Hargest, allowing contact
with their comrades south and east down the range
in Prison Valley. Under the impact
of these reverses Freyberg arranged
a fallback – defeat that was victory estranged

29

To its Antipodes in just three days.
The Chania coast must have reminded
Freyberg of Levin and of his trade
as dentist in that town, before he signed
up to the Royal Marines. A narrow line
of coastal plain – the Horowhenua
'shaky ground' like Crete – where forces resigned
themselves to the flat in a laminar
flow, while leaving the range to a liminary

29 – Horowhenua means 'shaky ground' in Māori. Both the Horowhenua district and the Gulf of Chania are extremely seismic.

30
  enemy hidden in gullies and slopes.
  Bishop Monrad, who settled in that town
  after the Schleswig war, could not cope
  with war parties that came raiding down –
  and retired to Denmark and sad renown.
  Just as during the Cook Strait War, George Grey
  realised an intercept would win him ground,
  if he sent troops in from the sea to stay
  a force, so Germans in the rear stalled Chania Bay.

31
  We have no playing fields of Eton
  no Waterloo. We learned our ways of war
  from wide Otaki, to trails beaten
  through the Tararuas. The flaw
  with a shallow plain is that a corps
  presents a front that is only a flank.
  Any gaps in the queue can be torn
  apart from air, sea, or mountain. The ranks
  then fold up and withdraw – defeat falls off one plank.

30 – Bishop Monrad was prime minister of Denmark during the second Schleswig war of 1864. He emigrated to Levin, which he left after a war party, or *taua*, alarmed him in 1868. Sir George Grey (1812–98) had to fight Ngati Toa and its war chief Te Rangihaeata in 1846 in the Horowhenua. He used a paddle steamer instead of Junkers and gliders.

32

    Ō daimōnie. Charles Upham walks
    the maze like in a lounge he has been
    in before. He does not even stalk
    the enemy – he comes to them unseen
    and avoids where their machine guns preen
    the air with fire. Tag – you're the minotaur.
    He is the only one not in the dream.
    3000 yards in – who else holds the floor?
    Walking into Maleme by an open door.

33

    Purgos has always meant 'tower' in Greek.
    Māori – now fighting for the Crown – retook
    the village of Pirgos at the peak
    of their counter-attack but would have looked
    in vain for towers. Their courage hooked
    response from General Julius Ringel's
    Gebirgsjäger. The Luftwaffe shook
    the ground between the shore's soft shingle
    and olive groves, over which the blue star Rigel

---

32 – Charles Upham VC and bar won his first VC for actions during the Battle of Crete, starting with the counterattack on Maleme on 22 May.
36 – There is such a toponym as Cydonia (the modern Chania) on Mars.

CANTO II

34

shone transparent in day. One foot forward
for Ringel, but *Puānga* – the presage
of the dawn – Pleiades and herald
of a new year, for Māori. The ages
have come to Crete, but such a fighting stage
as Māori raised close to the airfield
was quite new – their *pūwhara* maze and cage.
On Crete with its straight rivers and rich eels
their labyrinth, the *pā maioro*, stood revealed.

35

The Ju 87 is a scream
on wings, sent by Alexander Löhr.
A yelling harpy seems to be its theme.
Even the gulls are black on this shore
then our guys make themselves obscure.
For some there is joy beneath such hatred –
they carry on in the transfixing lure.
The Stuka is hard to underrate
even as it shrieks intention to devastate.

36

Cydonia is a place on Mars.
Minos founded it (some say Hermes),
which implies trade busied its two harbours –
one a roadstead – the other remedies
that with Souda Bay. Red anemones
are proper for the troops who never left
Merkur's polis. Whether calumnies
or truth, myth about the Allies has cleft
the memory of this last stand, turned facts into theft.

37

>Hermes has done his work of translation
>and commerce far too well, and cheated
>everyone in his market. Location
>trafficks in rumour's usury that greets
>all comers, then trolls on with incomplete
>skeletons of exhumed narrative.
>Even the Germans feel deleted
>and short-changed by the truth's fugitive
>horizon, as it sweeps the coast with privatives.

38

>Freyberg among the sandbags, watches
>battle. He looks like he has come to take
>the air, even as the Germans notch
>up results. Failure is a corpse to rake
>over, not to tend. Success forsakes
>itself as well, does not respond to grins
>of subsequently grateful men, who make
>him corona graminea, and spin
>the story of a learning curve, and chastened win.

39

>The downfall of an ancient city
>was a dreadful event, as some victors
>acknowledged. The Phaeacians felt pity
>for those at Troy – Virgil's Dido pictured
>its fall with compassion. Even lictor-
>led consuls professed to feel pathos
>for the city destroyed. In this sector
>at least – cities were spared. Without hubris
>we should throw a last party, turn on the bathos –

40

'You'll find a crazy place Daedalus built
at the heart of a little old Greek town.
You will be shown where all the blood's spilt
even on Tuesdays when us guys clown
about the town, until Jerry frowns
and the underworld meets the master race.
Oh – this is the place Jerry surrounds.
Come and meet these dancing feet in the place
which Mr Bull Man reckons is such a disgrace.

41

'We're the little nifties from the fifties
because this is 42nd Street.
We are the dancing feet and little nifties.
Jerry's those sexy ladies so indiscreet
who try out Souda Bay and get our fleet.
Come on, guys, we better get ornery –
tap dance a chorus with our nifty feet.
Come on Jerry – this naughty bawdy
gaudy sporty 42nd Street is horny.'

41 – On 27 May, Australian troops and the Māori Battalion carried out a spectacular and audacious bayonet charge in Chania against Gebirgsjäger of the 5th Alpine Division descending from the Chania Peninsula, called 'The Battle of 42nd Street', after the 1933 musical film and the song '42nd Street', which has been adapted here. The road fought for on this occasion had been named after the British 42nd Engineers who had camped there.

42

    The epic is a bath of cold-blooded
    bathos, like Minos in the steam room,
    and Agamemnon severed for a flood.
    The epic does its best to be a tomb
    and not a cenotaph. Active on Zoom
    the characters log into sessions
    revisit the past and try to resume
    where they left off. We hear confessions.
    We find some obdurate – still filled with obsession.

43

    Talos had broken down. The harbour
    was ablaze. Freyberg gave the order
    for evacuation. An armada
    waited at Sfakia: time to shoulder
    packs, cross the island that is a border
    in itself, learn its depth for escape,
    as Germans came on like marauders.
    A trail of dysentery and blood gaped
    ahead, if the force were to board in any shape.

44

    The Greek government and George II
    needed to be got out first in case
    the confusion left them jettisoned
    and taken as prizes. Then they faced
    departure from Sfakia – the base
    of Greek independence against the Turks
    in 1821, to be erased
    by Germany as a failed bulwark.
    Sfakia became Greece and New Zealand's Dunkirk.

45

The king with the cold eyes was respected
by the people at least as the sign
of a state that had been effective
against Italy, if not to define
a free future. Sfakia is the blind
end and brazier of a free Greece.
This signal burns in the heart, out of mind
to the world. Greece was unfurled from the crease
and tuck of time long after liberty had ceased.

46

Crete is a headboard of cliffs to the south.
Like the Old Man of Crete, it has fissures
cracks and narrow canyons, to the bright mouths
of streams, which precipitate and issue
into the Libyan Sea. Their depth is measured
by vultures' tight descent, and plummet
to the landing stage's last divesture.
Sfakia lies in the path of bullets.
Upham there made moves that made gods out of grommets.

46 – In Austral English a 'grommet' is a novice at a dexterous sport requiring balance, like surfing or skateboarding. Charles Upham VC held off a German descent onto Sfakia, while ill with dysentery and in a state of exhaustion.

47

None of this was ever Xenophon.
Thalassa thalassa. New Zealand lost
its Greece at Sfakia, but colophons
are not what we do. Headlong retreat costs
in ways, retreat in depth never solaced.
Freyberg in his command cave has a break.
Xenophon in shorts has poured the boss
a cuppa. This is the stage when men shake
from tiredness – Dikte's cave where the small nations quake.

48

Time to abandon Crete's parapet –
leave it to the Cretans and Germans.
Time to sail to hospital and Egypt –
to clear out bacteria and vermin.
Not yet time to absorb new lessons.
The body needs a grease and oil change.
Whoever sleeps the most will determine
the course of the war. No one arranges
a battle – it is self-organised derangement.

49

Each cloud has its inclination to rain.
Major Walter Koch comes to in the ward,
watches the sky's slope, and wonders how pain
was not enough to make men less forward,
at death's bloodstream he had just forded.
Perhaps it depends on how well one woke –
the angle of sleep where life was regained.
Still, propensity to crime was revoked.
In a rush of hard tyres and headlights – his storm broke.

50

Alexander Löhr who had planned Merkur
was shot after the war, while Student
was spared by Inglis. The only decor
these generals cared for had been pendent
and two-tone. Meindl looked resplendent
in Knight's Cross with Oak Leaves, but Swords veered
away from him at the last moment.
At Nijmegen he brought defeat nearer.
Gericke was promoted to the Bundeswehr.

51

A child does not know where sovereignty
comes from. It does not hatch out of bombs.
The fact is, New Zealand and Germany
once fought over it on Crete. Drop a rhumb.
It does not exist save in hecatombs
of the mind. Poetry never stopped
a tank, but it drove a few with aplomb.
Truth is something either helicoptered
from the future, or springs from the dragon-teeth crop.

---

49 – it is strongly suspected that Knight's Cross winner Colonel Walter Koch (1910–43), who commenced the action against Hill 107 at Maleme, was murdered by the SS in a car accident after refusing to carry out the Führerbefehl on Commandos on British commandos in Tunisia in a dispute with other officers, in which he expressed himself in language that deprecated Adolf Hitler.

52

Asterion performs his ministry
under the stars. He is the star dome
where meteors add to the mystery.
Up on the mountain he drives it home.
He has become God. The gift is on loan.
Use it or lose it. He commits the crime
he denies to others. He sends up drones
and satellites now to purchase time,
and weave the maze tighter with closer pattern and rhyme.

53

Virgil considered the horror of Crete.
In Georgics IV he contrasts the bounded
and unbounded, so they do not compete,
yet are distinct and unconfounded.
Such is the Lake of Darkness he sounded.
The god is one who infracts the limit,
refusing it to others, then re-grounds
it in law. For Virgil the state admits
its wrongdoing – works to law that is consummate.

54

The child cowering in the house afraid
of fire, will not know the State is sorry
someday down the line. People who had prayed
for deliverance, get out the lorries
and troop carriers' way in a hurry.
There are threads of hope that can be spun
which Virgil kept on spinning unworried –
those of love – to be broken or undone,
those of revolution which he saw overcome.

55
    The Cretans say there is a tomb of Zeus.
    Where it was, no one can identify.
    This was a myth the other Greeks traduced.
    The question is, was Zeus yet to die
    or was this tomb already occupied.
    Et le bunker était vide. Embargoed.
    Zeus died and died again disguised
    in bullshit – the maze is a farrago
    we have to live in. We shall forego
    Asterion's last words – *je me meurs – pas un mot.*

55 – I acknowledge quoting from Fabrice Bouthillon and Samuel Beckett.

Canto III

1

>The Expeditionary Force found a perch
>at Venice's Palazzo Dandolo.
>'The Stones of Venice' had once paved Christchurch,
>and inspired Francis Petre's Otago.
>Cafés called the Lido and Rialto,
>cinemas quite unlike the models
>Ruskin took from the Gothic long ago.
>In a doge's palazzo in huddles
>New Zealanders stand at the bar and get sozzled.

1 to **4** – please refer to the Orpheus and Eurydice myth in Virgil's *Georgics* IV, to Claudius Claudianus' *De raptu Proserpina*, and to Monterverdi's operas *Orfeo* and *Proserpina rapita*. The latter was premiered at the Palazzo Dandolo (now the Hotel Danieli) in 1630 for a Mocenigo-Giustinani wedding. Claudian lived c. 370–c. 404 CE, and Claudio Monteverdi lived 1567–1643. The British art critic and social thinker John Ruskin (1819–1900) is also referred to, and the New Zealand architect Francis Petre (1847–1918).

CRETE 1941

2

After more than four years of warfare,
they had battled their way from Greece to Crete,
from Egypt to the Maghreb, and shared
two years in Italy, to defeat
the Germans. Their ranks had been depleted.
It was April 1945.
The peace they made would never be complete,
nor the sorrow that had come alive
in many of them – pools of fear they had to dive.

3

The kingfisher knows how to reverse,
but these guys are scared they will not pull out.
They have to make grief a friend and rehearse
life all over again. The marabout
at the desert's edge – what was he about?
Only the woman who looked at one long
with never a smile, made silence shout.
Of the accidents of war, the strongest
is love: a surgeon's knife withheld or else prolonged.

4

The question was put by the Mantuan,
what was it that Orpheus sang to move
the underworld powers? Claudian
composed one answer from Milan which proved
his '*de raptu Proserpinae*' – truth
of what had moved Hades and his queen.
A later Mantua, and Venice, soothed
recollection, gave grief the chance to keen,
ravished by the music from Monteverdi's scenes.

CANTO III

5

'My death is closer to me than life' –
a soldier thinks in the hospital ward.
Never a vierge folle – she is now his wife,
while he her infernal spouse is restored,
but to what? For pain's conjugal chords
are performed on a silent piano
he alone follows, unless he gets bored,
not to be played loud from the radio
of his imprisoned body – from *Fidelio*.

6

The nurses have turned our war hero off.
He lies there and considers the pain.
Sickbeds in boyhood for flus and coughs,
despite the same sun and quiet, did not train
him for this. Perhaps being constrained
to be born compares – if so the pain harks
back to what was not his to retain.
Some wake up to Death's Furies Fates and Parques.
Hitler had woken thinking he was Joan of Arc.

4 to **7** – *Fidelio* is Beethoven's only opera, in which the imprisoned Florestan, rescued by Leonore disguised as Fidelio from the evil Pizarro.

CRETE 1941

7

Florestan is rescued – but by who –
for how long? Either a lifetime to learn,
or a consummation will ensue –
ardent and brief. The doctors discern
which cases are borderline – some turn
out surprises one way or the other.
It can come down to how much patients yearn
or say no, for whether they recover.
A man's mystery of his innermost lover.

8

Claudian's epic was never finished.
Monteverdi's last opera is lost.
The libretto survives its vanished
Eurydice. Kiwis had not the ghost
of an idea then, of music's utmost.
Opera is for poofters surely –
would have been the officers' bar-room boast.
Some to fall silent, recalling purely
a furtive embrace of its passion and fury.

9

Opera though is an invocation
of the human through three of the arts
of the sacred; music's combination
of drama, along with poetry's part:
poiesis, the mathematics of the heart.
Corporal Muldoon would have been Pentheus,
peering at the Maenads' anarchy,
at Ceres ripping up the tenuous
pines on Sicily, at anger that strenuous,

CANTO III

10

if Monteverdi had not been mislaid,
or Claudian's work had been more in vogue.
Some learned to want to hear music played,
that provided them with life's analogue,
let a priestess dispose of the rogues
and monsters, they suspected they might be.
good on Muldoon for trying to prorogue
the war, for working with calamity.
The voice's fountain as the source of sanity.

11

Goddesses reveal the migration
of new cults throughout the eastern Med.
For instance, Europa's navigation
from Tyre to Crete to Brussels, the spread
of Ceres and cereals embedded
in Claudian, to Etna from Cyprus.
While Britomart names the Auckland railhead –
Oread who fled Minos' hubris –
Herself an outraged refugee seeking redress.

9 - Sir Robert David Muldoon (1921-92) was controversially prime minister of New Zealand 1975-84. He was the last of our state economy heads of government. Cabaret and high opera contended for his attentions, while he had scorn for the arts as such. Also refer to Eurypides' *Bacchae* and to Claudian's *De raptu Proserpinae* III in this stanza.
11 - The Auckland transport hub is indeed the Britomart Centre, named after a Royal Navy vessel in fact.

12

Britomart who went in the 'Faerie Queene'
as Chastity's paladin, protects
the sleeping soldier, dreaming what it means
when one woman has him alone for sex
and he is the father of nations septs
clans and tribes. He is the Adonis
in the garden of Venus Genetrix
up to her tricks. Dormouse Priapus
as the progenitor of the pickled foetus.

13

Britomart might fix him up with a lass
from the suburbs when he gets back home.
The lass will prepare a Sunday repast
and bicker with his mother. Hooks and domes
will fasten eyes and studs, unless he roams
the streets for non-existent bars and clubs,
and the waves at the beach welter foam.
'You'd better settle down!' people will rub
it in. How so, when a life has become a stub,

12 – Book Three of Edmund Spenser's *Faerie Queene* is dedicated to Britomart and the theme of Chastity. 'The Garden of Adonis' appears in this book, in which Venus/Aphrodite has Adonis to herself. Crete's red anemones have been referred to in Cantos I and II.

14

and a prosthesis is bunged on the stump
of war? Her book *Safe marriage – a return
to sanity*, does not drain the sump
of misery in all cases, and earned
her disrepute. The last war's saint squirmed
in state-cast nets of ignominy,
the mistress of wild beasts a smashed herm.
There is no defence against calumny
in New Zealand: no way to live antinomy.

15

It is not Orpheus who harrows hell
alone, but women also have tamed
its fauna. Who is there who can quell
Hades, move worse-than-night to tears, to claim
somebody back, provoke a sense of shame,
if not Proserpina, paroled first?
That is what Orpheus really came
to say. Song is dolour that had to burst.
Silence is the drought where even tears parch and thirst.

14 – Refers to Ettie Rout, the New Zealand nurse who was decorated by France for her sexual safety work. Her work was appreciated by New Zealand troops but not by the government and New Zealand establishment.

16

What are we making myth do? No more
than we do ourselves. It is the natural
selection of stories for setting law,
apart from the state, or an actual
judge. Eurydice's case is non-factual,
but demonstrates we could never uphold
a pact with death. What is conjectural
is compliance – not that we can be sold
such a deal, whereby lives go into the billfold.

17

The frogs and mice caught in theomachy
are ingested in Hieronymus Bosch –
like human fare in that deipnosophy.
The mind is a monster imposing costs.
It is certain it has not yet lost
if it can shape patterns of violence
with greater intensity. The kibosh
can be put on any reliance
on theodicy, or some man-god alliance.

17 – Please refer to the *Deipnosophistae* of Athenaeus.

CANTO III

18

See see – where Faust's blood streams meteors
in the firmament. The wireless shakes
and blinks with defiance, as it careers
into static. The ear is then slaked
with Mozart's 'Magic Flute' before that breaks
into raspberries – Nimrod inserting
du blasphème as he misuses his stake
in the airwaves, should listeners revert
to 182 kHz.

19

Myth is this calm block that has been turned off.
Switch it back on for the cuckoo calls
to receive live an audience's coughs
and hear Papageno feeling small.
Tamino and Pamina never fall
once during their trials, having seen through
the Uranian queen. Touch that wall
with the ear, where those voices just blew
that are now dead, after grounding black flights and crew.

18 – Großdeutscher Rundfunk broadcast over Germany and much of Europe from Deutschlandsender I on 182 kHz.
19 – Please refer to Stéphane Mallarmé's – *Le tombeau d'Edgar Poe*. And Mozart's *The magic flute*.

20

> Then it is said the world will be renewed;
> we will go back to ordinary jobs,
> ordinary women – but without you
> who found me in the maze of war. I lobbed
> a grenade, then after heard Jerry sob
> and scream a bit. He would have done the same,
> but would Jerry have crouched down to rob
> me of my fags while still alive? I blame
> myself for frisking him still warm, and feeling shame.

21

> *Ernte 23s* taste red and orange
> I later shared them with the others.
> But kept his magic pills from my forage.
> I got stuck in and didn't just hover.
> I chucked his used *Gummi-Schutz* cover
> away – and some Hitler matchbox brand.
> I did this in no time – without any bother
> and made sure I got none of him on my hands.
> Another seemed dead: on a bare wrist – a watch ran.

20 – Iliad XXII 396 ff when Achilles despoils Hector, also at XXIII 21.
21 – Here we have Achilles' despoliation of Hector, combined with observance of the taboos that Diomedes violated, in Canto I and in *Aeneid* II.
Ernte 23s were a brand of German cigarettes, in red and orange packets. Ernte means 'harvest' but the tobacco then seems to have come from Greece. A New Zealander of that period would have pronounced 23 in English. The tablets were Pervitin tablets or methamphetamines, while the tin had been a condom container. Hitler appeared on quite a few matchboxes of the period.

CANTO III

22

    He thinks something closer than death has left
him to the chances of war – imagined
as a woman he sensed near. That theft
of a man still alive, will chagrin
him until death. There is no region
in the world, where he can get away
from that dying man, and what had bargained
for him. Who this rescuer is – in play
until she renders one up – is never betrayed.

23

    Why pass the mountain of water – mountain
of fire – to be a murderer and thief.
Gone is the word. The radio maintains
the silence, of never having relieved
the ears of that burden. Wounds or grief
would be progress of some kind, but the corpse
of sound is a fact beyond belief.
When it is switched on, sense is more thwarted
than stunned by blank silence, at which ear and eye gawp.

24

    The male mind's shadow or figuration
makes men harder to live with perhaps.
Hear Eurydice's recriminations,
or real-life Ariadne collapsed
in rage and sorrow on the beach. Love-maps
claim to be the treasure maps of Eros.
Our other half does a victory lap,
then waits for us to reach the terminus,
by which time tortoise is no longer amorous.

25

    Or else we hit the spot, squandering
    the troves of love's riot. War makes the chart
    more legible as soldiers wander
    the land in reiteration. Women start
    from different premises; they have three hearts
    or so that are more honest. Just the man
    is possessed. He finds himself one part
    of her life, and there are secrets he plans
    the peace round, if he is to feel that peace began.

26

    Ariadne rescued us from the maze
    and its burning minotaurs. Ungrateful
    for the risks she took, we enact replays
    of the enemy – battle's jackal
    anthropoid – with all the typing pool,
    or colleagues at the office or neighbours.
    War was another life inimical
    to lives thereafter. The right behaviour
    for veterans is placing youth in the sepulchre.

27

    Venice is a labyrinth on top
    of the mountain of water. Ariadne
    is a mariner, and has developed
    wisdom in men from her parody
    of Minos' scuole and seminaries.
    Time runs in a curve like the Grand Canal.
    Futures masquerade as anarchies,
    where young Andreas sinks in Hofmannsthal
    past madonnas and courtesans by intervals.

28
Dandolo – Dedalo. Venice got Crete
when Byzantium was divvied up.
New Zealand will remain incomplete,
a rude Serenissima – corrupt
from deliberate ignorance. The doo-wop
is now all the rage, and there are no girls
to do it with. The ideal city sups
on fish 'n' chips with oysters and streets furled.
Its fishermen will never become admirals.

27 – The *scuole* of Venice resembled the livery hall institutions of London. They were religious fraternities that served as think-tanks and training institutes for the Venetian ruling class and officials.
The eminent Austrian writer Hugo von Hofmannsthal (1874–1929) left a most intriguing incomplete novel *Andreas oder die Vereinigten*, set in the Venetian 18th century.
28 – Dandolo was the doge of Venice who instigated the Sack of Byzantium in 1204 and the division of the Byzantine empire that fell into the hands of the distracted IVth Crusaders. 'Dedalo' is Italian for Daedalus.
The Doo-wop is a temporal device because as a style of music and associated dance, it had begun by the 1940s, but only got its name when the vogue was passing, in 1961, the year I was born.

29
    But Salò's 120 days
    are over. We saved the survivors
    of the boys and girls from the fascist maze.
    We saved them from the flesh – its pearl-divers.
    The shock was that orgies were provided
    for, and calculated as counterpoint
    of cruelty and pleasure. Eliding
    such knowledge, of live bodies served as joints
    of beef and lamb, proved impossible for ointments

30
    And pills, catheters and cauteries,
    curettage to get rid of. Slaughterhouse
    secrets were Pentheus' quarterly
    resort. Meanwhile plucked naked as a goose,
    Admiral Canaris met the hangman's noose.
    Power is a parade ground and catwalk,
    where honour and dishonour arouse
    the worm of conscience: treason. Poor forked
    creature, reliant on far too much park-bench talk.

---

29 – Refer to Pasolini's film *120 Days of Sodom* (1975) at your own risk.
30 – Admiral Wilhelm Canaris (1887–1945) head of the *Abwehr* (German Military Intelligence) 1935–44, was executed in April 1945.

CANTO III

31

    The Grand Canal is a perspective
    of quays boatsheds boathouses and stilts,
    made into death's dazzle, the reflective
    passages dangerous for their built
    immunity to tide and sewerage silt.
    Mithridatised city of Mercury
    quick and cold, where dying became a quilt
    and bed of broken glass, that matched Turkey
    with the Gothic, end-of-life physic with surgery,

32

    financial services and tontines.
    The future glimpsed in the walls and floors
    of time's curve, was not lads learning lanteens
    on the lagoon, but the state offshore:
    an automated revolver door.
    People who occupy these stage-sets,
    occupy a broken bucentaur.
    New Zealand only held this parapet
    and Crete, from learning how to be a surrogate.

33

    The mountain of fire had beaten us.
    Monte Cassino – a strange paladin
    among the Germans too. The US
    delivered air strikes worse than Ghibelline –
    burnt the monastery as a victim
    for our own safety. No one had counted
    Fridolin von Senger und Etterlin
    as a seraph. Salamanders amount
    to nothing in that fire. Not Freyberg on the mount,

34

    but Polish Catholics after the third
    battle, despite the artillery park
    we had deployed. The Allies had erred
    against a man whom Hitler had marked
    with disfavour. A clear flame in the dark
    is the bare limit. It cannot be touched.
    The enemy was a harlequin stark
    black and white – he was an eclipse of such
    extent – light burned on the rim or hid in a hutch.

33 & 34– Fridolin von Senger und Etterlin (1891–1963) was the German general who defended the German positions during the three Battles of Monte Cassino. He was a German of probity, a man of Catholic civilisation (when that still existed). Hitler disliked him to the extent that he downgraded the 'Gustav Line' to the 'Senger Line' to make it sound expendable. No war crimes were charged against him, nor were ever alleged – in fact he prevented them.
The Ghibellines were the Imperial party in the conflicts of the 13th century opposed to the pro-papal Guelfs. It is not that the Americans were anti-Catholic in 1944. They had no sensitivity, and they got it wrong. General von Senger observed a pact not to militarise the site.

35

    Deluded Trivelin still wears patches
that are light. Scaramouche is camouflaged
in regulated horror. Snatches
of Papageno die out on the marge
of unconfounded night. What is at large,
is the Plutonian anthropoid.
Persuading it lay beyond our charge.
Let Orpheus probe the lightless void,
that comes about, if civility is destroyed.

36

    Hermann Broch speaks on the radio,
foretelling the death of the poet
live from a Viennese studio.
Virgil was no longer the pilot
and apotropaic amulet
on the lake of darkness, where on one bank
power stays abortive and inchoate,
while on the other, puts lights on point blank
at the landing stage, where arrivals thought they sank

37

    deepest at their disembarkation,
after their descent across death's liquid
core. But no – they made new incarnations
which barely lived – in a zone of solid
misery, if not ash for the turbid
air. In his office as Orpheus,
Virgil fails. Information leaks squalid
and pale from out of a Möbius
strip – the surface of which keeps das Man amorphous.

38

Leaving Augustus at Rome's Cloaca,
Virgil does not shut down Ixion's wheel.
At his approach – hell gets even darker
instead of *refrigerium's* brief deal
with song. Those are judges beyond appeal,
worse than Minos and Rhadamanthus.
This phantasmagoria is too real,
for finding Tiresias the mantis
or Eurydice, serve their terminal sentence.

39

Labyrinths are where humans are corralled,
and minotaurs are never distracted.
From Antipolis, no-one is paroled,
since Acheron is the cataract
of Lethe, dissolving the bonds for pacts.
Someone's death is impossible to sound,
despite the potential for speech acts.
In a new way we are back to old ground
Eurydice of course is nowhere to be found.

40

Before Proserpina, he might display
the best singing and insist that our souls
are – *d'una buia prigion ...uscite*.
Elysium is in the Reich's control
however, whether Leon Blum on hold
from Vichy, or Papagos at Dachau.
This cold-shouldered Spring is going to foal
no new horses. From the Rhine to Breslau
watch the Lyrids fall, and the Queen of Night uncowed.

41

There is no point being *ad feminam*
with her – *Proserpina rapita è*
and now death has become her demonym.
The enemy moved beyond simile,
wince we were defeated at Maleme.
The girl in a dungeon in Ceres' dream,
was once Demeter's lost Persephone.
Claudian granted her a rising theme
to the government of everything that had been.

42

Infamy has many names – Josie Brock,
Irma Grese, Johanna Altvater.
Many had been trained at Ravensbrück.
For his broadcast, Broch knew for starters
that Virgil had nothing to barter,
and that the Mantuan had averted
Orpheus' fate. The song is pro-rata'd
at bottom rate, as the poet inverts
the song contest, making poetry an advert.

43

The myth had broken down on all fronts.
Virgil had to escape empty-handed.
Orpheus was interned, gave no account
of his song before he was banded
with others and killed. Virgil demands
that we know this can happen. The ifs
in Georgics IV only make their landing
so as to measure evil's azimuth.
What if the Prince does not accept the incentive

44

    to acknowledge his crime to Eurydice,
    or some poet tries the song? Thrice-mentioned
    the Mantuan departs like in Dante.
    The Prince's rejection proves intention
    to total war. The poet's abstention
    refuses the beauty of evil,
    arising from Claudian's pretension,
    and wild flowers sprout quiet and idle.
    What Orphic song was should not be for retrieval.

45

    It was between a man and the death,
    he and his lover shared. Words cannot speak
    for a scar or mouth a wound – so be loath
    to break in. It was a meteor's streak
    anyway – sorrow's blazing tear that leaked
    in from the void. Such a fire is dew
    compared to our violence – not from antique
    emotion. Leave them standing in the blue.
    Meadow flowers that we should never pick and strew.

46

    Poppies for Demeter, the white poppies
    for Orpheus, and red anemone.
    Sorrow will never find its copy,
    it is enough to name the doubly
    lost daughter and that sure enemy
    to peace: a young man. Think of the fingers
    that move through the grasses, stubbornly
    searching for any traces that string
    along hope, or of some fate that is singular.

47

    Blanchot at his Èze persisted with myth,
insisting Eurydice was erased.
Subjectivity then a scream-queen cliff
hanger for girls, except Maurice unfazed
let them all drop. The poet's sovereign gaze
either means that the poet exists,
and lovers cease to be when out of phase,
or the poet dies. Then language persists
without the poem – and captives turn terrorist.

48

    The Lady of the Labyrinth gets jars
of honey, reads Linear B.
da-pu2-ri-tojo po-ti-ni-ja, scars
say on hard clay. There is no myth to see
in that, save some dignitary
at Knossos, or a goddess – her cult.
Forget men and boys and bulls: Ariadne
had the glamour, and not by default.
But try waiting for the snakes on her arms to moult.

---

47 – Maurice Blanchot (1907–2003) the French philosopher dwelt at Èze near Nice.

48 – The Mycenaean Greek is conjectured to translate from Linear B to read something like 'Lady of the Labyrinth' – *potnia laburunthoio*.

49

    That leaves the memory of Adonis,
and red anemones as reminders.
With age it is hard to get a focus
on who he was – the gestures that defined
the young man. I really doubt I could find
him at an identity parade,
or recognise his body. I still mind
what I feel; love at least was not delayed.
He was beautiful, as no future was betrayed.

50

    The flamethrower does its evil work.
Lord Chandos – his rats' nest burns. Wrinkled skin
stuck to flame, and the entire bulwark
shouts a moment. Bodies at the back skimmed
of air. It has taken this to win.
The radio announced Hitler is dead
now the battle for Austria opens
unless they surrender. How burned men fled
and fell – none of this, as Chandos wrote, can be said.

---

49 – A woman in later life reminisces here.

50 – The Italian of Giulio Strozzi's lyrics for the lost Monteverdi Opera matches Claudian's dream sequence for Ceres. 'Our souls have escaped from a dark and dirty prison'.

CANTO III

51

The soldier stirs in his bed. The nurses
look anxious all the time. His case is touch
and go; meanwhile his mind rehearses
the languages he has heard, which nourished
his senses with vivid words, which he clutched
at context to understand. Does he stay
in the wide world, or does he go and crouch
in a suburb? Either he finds the way
home again, or remains in the beautiful maze.

52

His mates have breakfast in the dining room
at the Danieli, then go over
the carless town once more. They assume
the pleasures of getting lost, these rovers
of the shy back channels. Words hover;
do they land? The mute pigeon memory,
will graze certain spots under the cover
of shade's disquiet and mystery.
Bright sea-water is the only directory.

---

51 – Hugo von Hofmannsthal's famous *The letter of Lord Chandos* on the futility of poetry and inadequacy of language.

53

    Venice is the former Atlantis
the mart of tinge and tang and taste walls,
in Helle and erthe and Paradis,
and each of them yards and courts and halls
in the sea. Some Daedalus built these stalls
and watercourses. The labyrinth's germ
of legend continually recalls
its portability. New Zealand's turn
will produce beach and suburb and motorway berm.

54

    The epic has to remain unfinished,
the opera lost as its heroine,
the harrowing of hell be diminished
to one-liners, which bear the gravamen
of our continual plaint. Pheromones
lead the soldiers to the discipline
of the housewife family and mortgage.
Their kits though contain personal baggage,
and bring back things unwritten in any language.

55

    The opera ends with Magna Graeca
with Cyprus, Sicily, Hellas and Crete,
far from Rome and Venice's cloaca.
Both Theseus and Ariadne cheat
each other at Asterion's defeat –
his labyrinth now just broken plinths.
Myth is death, yet nations keep repeating
it, till we are stuck in Crete's gore and lymph.
Heaven, though, is a mustard tree and terebinth.

Canto IV

1

Mycenae is the hot stone at his feet.
Knossos is the colony of ants,
which keeps circulating and repeating
labyrinths. Zeus is a gecko scant
upon the wall, Apollo the descant
from all cicadas, the goddesses. Blooms
the bees attend, while the occupant
beneath the boulder, is justice looming
as a small scorpion – Minos avoiding doom.

2

The Cretan poet lives outside of myth.
He is Daedalus, often an exile.
His genealogy runs in riffs
of No-one son of Nobody, smiled
on by none of the bug plant and reptile
gods. The waves do a little thunder.
The birds keep away from the scorching tiles.
Poetry is the end of wonder;
it is the garden cracked and broken asunder.

3

The ideal state is a partisan
unit. There men and women are held
in common for arms. These artisans
of revolution leave their caves to geld
the old god again, and start to herald
a new golden age, with people's courts
and public dining. Monsters must be quelled
among great powers, for Germans were taught
the perfect state existed in classical thought.

4

Myth is the monster the ideal state kills.
Obdurate story games the worst features
of mind, as an abattoir of spills
entertains the new Minotaur's creatures.
This is why each man and woman reaches
for a gun – this is why they look past
the Germans to organise the future.
The occupation has changed things fast.
Revolution is deliverance that can last.

5

So it seems. The poet's part is to call
on Nemesis, support Archidamus
on the mountain. Mesomedes installed
retribution as a theme; Rhianus
condemned Sparta's breaking and harnessing
of Messenia for heavy draught
and grain. In a later age Solomos
woke lightning's voice, with reverence and craft.
The bowman Elytis saluted sun with shafts.

6

This Greek is set against Latin, Turkish
and German. It is not Byron's helmet.
It is crossed cartridge belts, not a cuirass;
resisting Horace and the calumet
Hölderlin's carpenter smoked. Pelmetted
Knossos is nothing to Britomart's block,
which Daedalus carved, planed and celibate
at Olous. This Greek of Crete is such stock –
sweet virgin of hunting nets ambushes by shock.

5 – Poets of Crete are listed here. Mesomedes was a court poet of the Emperor Hadrian, who composed hymns to Nemesis. Rhianus lived in the 3rd century BCE and wrote an epic on the Messianian resistance under its last king, Archidamus, to Spartan conquest, in the Second Messenian War in the late 7th century BCE. Dionysios Solomos (1798-1857), the father of modern Greek poetry, belonged to a family of exiles from Crete, while Odysseus Elytis (1911-96) was born in Heraklion.

6 –The long pipe which Hölderlin's landlord and 'minder' brought with him to smoke beside the poet in psychotic silence, is compared to an American First Nations calumet or 'peace pipe'.

Hewn but featureless *xoana* or statues of an archaic kind were attributed to Daedalus. Britomart, whom we met in Canto III, had one at Olous on Crete. Ancient authorities say her name mean 'sweet virgin' in the ancient language of the island. She was a mountain nymph and chaste huntress like Artemis. It is said she invented hunting nets.

7

Crete does not have a Mt. Soracte.
General Kreipe – Knight's Cross minus Oak Leaves –
meant himself, name-dropping names *cum lacte*
learned when imperial languages teethes.
Patrick Leigh Fermor joined in relieving
him of partisan presence, in a game
that blocked third parties. I am a peak sleeved
and mantled in white: you boys go and claim
your youth and love, as if you can put me to shame.

8

'This calls for champagne all round!' – Kreipe's staff
celebrate their general's kidnap, then plan
reprisals. Horace made dire epitaphs.
It is torture to die just to be spammed
for one's country. Hölderlin is a gram
of crystal meth all in a bad cause.
This Orcus keeps both a slice and a dram
of the divine, brought to ground with its flaws.
Zeus-impersonators cut off their fathers' balls.

---

7 – Major General Heinrich Kreipe (1895-1976) was kidnapped on 26 April 1944 on Crete by British commandos led by Patrick Leigh Fermor and Greek partisans. Kreipe quoted Horace's Ode I.9 and Fermor completed the lines.
8 – Read *Der Archipelagus* of Hölderlin. Zeus overthrew and castrated his father Kronos.

CANTO IV

9

No one is Conchis in this. The British
invented Mr. Conchis to indulge
their love of masque, whereby they skirmish
with memory, flip out of Malebolge,
even as other nations divulge
their deaths of tragedy. Cretans went through
this long ago – the cloud black or fulgent
for them, not just grey; which is how they crew
a ship all can join, tell a story all find true.

10

Once again – the Cretans are the people
of the *Erotokritos*. Ages are brought
into communion; medieval
ancient and Renaissance tropes reported
at Athens, as love's ultimate court.
Ferrara in Candia – not Ireland,
patient Griselda's Midsummer – wrought
out of matinades and contraband.
My love a lit candle that went out in my hands.

9 – Reference to John Fowles, *The Magus*. The Malebolge is a place in Dante's *Inferno* VIII. It is also an esoteric programming language.

10 – The *Erotokritos* of Vitsentzos Kornaros (1553–1613/14) is the epic of Crete, largely set at a royal court in Athens. It is an amazing poetic and musical experience. It contains a 'Patient Griselda' theme and reminds one of the human actors in *A Midsummer Night's Dream*.

11

Partisan captains out of that epic,
led the Cretan resistance, to drive
Germans into the sea. The proleptic
island found in Mesara one, who thrived
in making the fightback come alive.
Giorgios Petrakis, a landowner
outgeneralled the Germans in striving
to recover the land, the donor
of all he that had, occupation's re-zoner.

12

The eagle of Psiloritis ran
an olive oil business, 'Selfridges'
in Cretan. The Greek resistance began
with competition for the ridges,
to fight the Axis from, and no bridges
between local capital and labour.
Tobacco and olive oil privileged
one class over its working neighbours,
got in the way of resisting the invaders.

11 & 12 – Giorgios Petrakis (1890–1972) was an outstanding partisan leader in the Greek resistance aligned with the EOK. Named 'the eagle of Psiloritis', he controlled the Mt Ida region and operated in the east and southeast of Crete. His code name for the British Special Operations Executive was 'Selfridge' after the Canadian-British department store chain, on the grounds that his olive oil factory was the Cretan equivalent of Selfridges.

CANTO IV

13
>Crete had been Venice's sad Azores
>or Caribbean isle, where cotton
>exhausted the ground, and sugar cane bored
>for water. Spuds did not go rotten
>at Lassithi, nor had Turks forgotten
>tobacco. Wasteland translates as *guasto*.
>This new world had been misbegotten
>on the old – a land Zoroaster
>would ken, the dust too level to be impasto.

14
>A desert for cacti, and paradise
>for thyme the luminous bees feed on,
>it had the workforce and defeudalised
>peasants to match, and organisation.
>Maybe Clinias' constitution
>could be built by a mountain government.
>Plato's 'Laws' seemed a revolution –
>Marx an implement not an improvement,
>to reach the bee and cactus flower covenant.

---

13 – *Inferno* XIV.26 on Crete.

15

> Pendlebury, Woodhouse and Fermor
> had wanted George II (the Third)
> restored; for the briefest of tenures
> as it turned out. Rural parts deferred
> to the nocturnal council, let its word
> hold through EAM and its army ELAS.
> To the judgeships of Minos, they referred
> those leaders popular and zealous:
> Michaelis Samvitis and Giannis Podias.

16

> The old god sleeps inside the mountain,
> some lost king. The communists are that now.
> The old man of Crete is a fountain
> of this discord's three rivers, of the rows
> between red Phlegethon, the white vow
> of Styx, and blue Acheron. Lethe runs
> Anapodiaris, disallowing
> recollection. The mouth it had won
> debouches on the political maze re-spun.

16 – There is a River Anapodiaris on Crete that flows into the Libyan sea – a long one. The whole point of Dante's Old Man of Crete is that Lethe is not one of the underworld rivers issuing from the fissure in the Old Man. Consider what *anapodiaris* means. In 'Der Ister', Hölderlin says: *'Der scheinet aber fast/ rückwärts zu gehen'*.

17 – Melpomene is the Muse of Tragedy.

17

Crete is turned into a labyrinth
of partisans against the enemy.
The young men tear up their hyacinths;
women refuse to be Melpomene,
take up arms against the hegemony;
old men take it in the gut and survive.
Of dreadful deaths endured, wounds remedied,
guerrilla armies do not keep archives.
This intensity kills or dies when kept alive.

18

George Psychoundrakis was a maze-runner;
like Pheidippides he had seen Pan.
The Cretan 5th Division late summer
after the invasion finished, began
to return demobilised – each man
to a home no longer his own. Gendarmes
like Manolis Paterakis ran
the hazards of a bandit's life – the arm
of the law outside law, just as upright and calm.

---

18 – George Psychoundrakis (1920–2006) was a legendary resistance fighter and runner like the famous Pheidippides c. 490 BCE. He also wrote on the Cretan resistance. He and Manolis Paterakis were involved in the Kreipe kidnapping. Herodotus VI 105-106 is the source for Pheidippides' career and his meeting the god Pan.

CRETE 1941

19

    Dudley 'Kiwi' Perkins used the sickle
    against one parent culture of the west.
    He enters the Akritic cycle,
    because he said yes to Crete's call to rest
    on Crete forever. One of the best
    of the partisan leaders, till given
    over to ambush, we have to confess
    him one of our private men, driven
    to find other New Zealands – raised up and riven.

20

    Young Doundoulakis wakes up and finds
    himself the Minotaur. What a party –
    laid girls, dead Germans and broken blinds,
    ephebes needing to detox, heartily
    sick of having to act out a brat's part;
    sunken ships and burned airfields to cope
    with forever. Asterion was smart –
    he built a radio telescope
    with his brother, broke with the Earth heliotrope.

---

19 - Dudley Churchill 'Kiwi' Perkins (1915–44) of Christchurch, New Zealand, lived on Crete a year after the Battle of Crete and learned Greek before being evacuated to Egypt. He chose to return and led his own partisan group. The Akritic cycke is a Byzantine cycle of border songs of the warring between Muslims and Christians in eastern Asia Minor a millennium ago. *Digenes Akrites* is the major epic of this cycle.

20 & 21 - The brothers George Doundoulakis (1921-2007) and Helias Doundoulakis (1923-2016) of Heraklion were Greek Americans who worked

CANTO IV

21
    They listened to the stars, to the tuning
    fork sounds of the planets, leaving the planes
    at Kastelli and fuel dump long fuming.
    Schoolboy friends ensured the traitor was slain
    who tried to blackmail the pair, reclaimed
    by torpedo boat for espionage.
    Asterion began the killing chains –
    Daedalus started on sabotage.
    The labyrinth insists on one-way arbitrage,

22
    like the paramour who divulged details
    of a convoy, or risky abortions.
    The hero can go into retail,
    aerospace, or banking as his portion
    in life. Women underwent extortion
    and torture too. Their resilience
    did not come from rebound and torsion,
    but poured from a fountain's salience
    in Agia Dynami's cool ebullience.

---

with the British SOE on Crete and with the American OSS in Greece. They became physicists and engineers, and designed the Arecibo radio telescope in Puerto Rico.

22 – Agia Dynami are the springs at Agyroupoli above Retimno. 'Holy power' or 'holy force' is the meaning.

23

'We toil through a mighty maze' intoned
Churchill – 'but I assure the committee
it has a plan'. Minos, it seemed, was prone
to communism. The just city
erred towards 'mental instability',
averred reports, as Podias feuded
with Manolis Bandouvas. Amity
became outrage as brave captains brooded
on vengeance : are the Brits and Germans colluding?

24

The thrush loses its thread back to the tree
it nested in. It has no need of such
knowledge in its maze of liberty.
Seferis' 'Thrush' was a wreck retouched
with Baudelaire's swan, and the weak sun clutched
at by a coughing woman. How yellow
was his wagtail – white beneath very much,
like his flycatcher's horizon. Hello
real brown thrush, true light is black and never sallow.

23 – This is an allusion to the claim that Communists were a common enemy for both the Germans and British. Certainly, Chania remained under armed German control, with the permission of the British, after the capitulation on 9 May 1945. There was no VE Day for Crete. This stanza alludes to a quicksand of allegations regarding SOE policy for Crete and how Manolis Bandouvas might have been 'set up'. The Communists had an interest in protecting villages from reprisals, as these were the basis of their 'mountain government' on Crete.

24 – I refer to George Seferis' great poem 'Thrush' (1946) and connect with

CANTO IV

25

    The world is not the egg and quince-tree nest,
coherent though they seemed, not the wreck
abandoned to the sea. The thrush's quest
tree after tree remains symmetric
with its needs. The sole reality-check
it gets is death, always particular
to itself. It sees in dark shade and flecks
of light, avoiding the spectacular,
except when it sings Philomel's vernacular.

26

    We cannot see just in black and white.
We must learn to look in light that is black,
as Asterion does beneath the fright
of stars. Whose enemy do we attack
Greece's, or Britain's next cataract
down its river – a cold Crimean war?
That Christians are communists might attract
disbelief, but Crete wants to devise law
for itself. The island is its own warrior.

Charles Baudelaire's *Le cygne*. The 'thrush' of Seferis' poem is a masted shipwreck, while real wagtails and flycatchers feature in the poem. Two kinds of wagtails can be seen in Greece; without indulging in ornithology, I opt for the white variety, because of Seferis' line about the sunset, which notes the 'golden keg' is depleted.

25 – In myth Philomel got turned into a nightingale, but a song thrush is known as 'turdus philomelos'. It is often mistaken for a nightingale.

27
    Borderlands have been poetry's sites
    for making dual identities clear.
    Digenes Akritas has a fight
    with a lion, a dragon and two bears,
    a hind – his father had been an emir.
    He carried off a general's daughter
    and made love to an Amazon compeer;
    the hind had been torn in its slaughter.
    A palace on the Euphrates were his quarters.

28
    A severed head and speared-through body
    belongs with Herakles, to Bacchus
    the ripped hind. Rivers turn into wadis,
    myth drains into chivalry, the cactus
    of spaghetti westerns. Such practices
    reveal the absence of Priam, to weep
    and gather the remains. The prospectus
    of war's horrors is tragedy's sweep
    of the temple yard, where the worst will soon be heaped,

29
    and strangely discharged to our wonder.
    Then the yard will be purified and swept
    again. On Crete what is the yonder?
    Where the sails and wings of enemies leapt
    from the horizon, where allies crept
    in and out again? Migrants return
    from America totally adept
    at technology and business; to spurn
    tragedy however – their memory interned.

30

The massacre at Viannos started
with assurances. Come down from the hills.
We mean you no harm. We are kind-hearted
young guys. Then males 16+ were killed –
the mountain's lap was torched and fire milled
their harvest to ash. After the landings
on Sicily, Bandouvas brought peril
to Viannos, striking an outpost stranded
on the Libyan sea – the best care notwithstanding.

31

A split mountain stands red-tinged nearby,
its ravine a nasty wound that proves
one earthquake could tear a range, and ply
it apart like a hind. The obscene groove
is worse for looking fresh – an œuvre
these Eteo-Cretans once insisted
they witnessed. Nothing will ever smooth
such rupture as long as the mountain exists;
nor in that plane tree, where the town runs out of twists.

---

31 – This landscape is to be found at Viassos.

32

Friedrich-Wilhelm Müller came from Barmen
Wuppertal. *Mein Herze schwimmt im Blut*
but *Büß und Reu* never oozed as balm
for one so *ungeheuer*. He would put
villages to death that wrong-footed
his Festung-Kreta and its labour draft,
make them corpses of rubble and soot.
He practised war as a limitless craft –
'The Butcher of Crete' has become his epitaph.

33

The hero of the Bug river bridge,
the re-conqueror of Feodosia,
did more than a military carnage.
Pomegranate blood was ambrosia
to him on Crete – he wore insignia
for torture, not just the field of battle.
Though the Wehrmacht had been his clothier
and outfitter, Ajax taught him cattle
and livestock cuts, one shriek short of a death rattle.

---

32 – General der Infanterie (Lieutenant General) Friedrich-Wilhelm Müller (1897–1947) was a more than competent general who resorted to torture and massacre on Crete. I refer to the Bach Cantata BWV 199: 'My heart swims in blood' is what the German says. *Ungeheuer* is in the cantata too and refers to the monstrosity which a sinner or criminal becomes. '*Büss und Reu*' (repentance and remorse) is from St Matthew's Passion. The verbs *barmen/erbarmen* denote having pity and showing mercy, regardless of the etymology of the toponym.

Müller was awarded the Knight's Cross with Oak Leaves and Swords. He had

34
> This is why small nations had to fight.
> The strangest labyrinth is the maze
> of the self, when we arrive out of sight
> of who we have been, and think that new phase
> is knowledge. Friedrich the Great challenged traits
> of the Prince in 'Anti-Machiavel'.
> Subjects themselves adopt evil ways,
> when the kingdom is ruled bedevilled
> by the Prince, if servants act at the same level.

35
> Prerogative monopolises this,
> says it imposes the limit later.
> A whole state is tainted by the promise,
> that citizens should have immolated
> their share of enemies. The satyr
> calls out to his fellow, the Minotaur
> grinds his hoof. He is domesticated
> by the labyrinth, in so far as war
> keeps him localised to the abattoir floor.

distinguished himself as a field commander by capturing the Bug River bridge intact in 1941, and by recapturing Feodosia in Crimea, after General Han Graf von Sponeck had lost it. He ended his military career surrendering in East Prussia to the Red Army. He was extradited to Greece where he was tried and convicted of war crimes on Crete, for which he was sentenced to death by firing squad.

34 – Friedrich II of Prussia published his *Anti-Machiavel* in 1740, edited by Voltaire. Rousseau dedicated Book III of *Du contrat social* to *The prince*.

35 – The satyr comes from the King James translation of Isaiah 13.

CRETE 1941

36

To axion esti – that the axe bit,
that the hardened steel scalpel did its work,
that the bitter bird of a chisel lit
on my face, to dig out my eyes, which irk
your glance. On this isle, evil has no murk
and arrives unannounced, barely shading
the clear day. I am holes that do not shirk
the need to feel, the seer abraided
the spokesman muted, the source of life invaded.

37

The elm is green that Virgil spoke of.
The abandoned village passed it by,
to mountains halfway to the moon above
in blue void of the late morning sky –
refugees making for Magnesia nigh.
The polis is setting out for a site,
to replace the one that had to die.
Surely, they will reach it before night,
village abandoned to Stukas and dynamite.

---

36 – Odysseus Elytis' poem *To axion esti* (It is worthy).

38

In response to Petrakis' feats
Müller had sent Stukas to dive-bomb
Vorizia – the Guernica of Crete.
We may call that village a hecatomb,
but what does that mean. It was a bosom
blown open, close by that gash. The cave
of Kamares – long-healing, where sombre
and solemn, the people have behaved
as if before gods, seeking some way to be saved

39

since Minoan and neolithic times.
That was before Viannos – why then provoke
Müller further? Into the cave their crimes
and desires are poured, the walls are soaked
with woe and rue. Their small voices stroke
the humid ear – that seismic eardrum.
At such a place, the need for language pokes
at nothing and nothing's pushback dumb
allows tears and promises, rejects chrysostom.

---

38 – The razing of Vorizia occurred on 23 August 1943. The cave of Kamares was a votive site in Minoan times, as is shown by offerings of Kamares ware ceramics from c. 1700 BCE found there. George Petrakis' band made their oaths of loyalty at the cave in 1941.

CRETE 1941

40

    Kriti is the land of the kri-kri,
the first of domesticated goats,
long wild again. Males are called agrimi;
the females sanada. Antelopes
are what they look like, in fawn and black coats,
yet the kids resemble lambs and sheep.
They rest on the heights and gaze at the coasts –
long-horned agrimi that fence on the steep
delicately, with their crescents grown back in sweeps.

41

    Partisans fed on them till 200
were left. Now they thrive in large numbers.
The guests at some cost became kindred
to the kri-kri. Fear rose and stark wonder,
not at Germans but a man in umber,
where there is no maze in which to run
save timber never made into lumber.
They appeared to Germans in the sun
armed with Enfields SVT 40s and Sten guns.

42

    By 1944 Dudley Perkins
had thoroughly assimilated Pan.
He did not join Lord Rakehell, Jack Jargon
and Hughe Develdrive's revived Medmenham,
at 'Tara' on the Nile. The programme
of violence carried out by 'Vassili'
was the resistance of a partisan,
not the rearguard action of a Kiwi
still continuing the battle of Maleme.

43
   The black light has risen on the land.
   It came so the white light was its shadow.
   Perkins could see it clearly as his hand –
   fingers palms and wrists never widowed
   of their will, to stalk wildflower meadows
   the hillsides and ridges for any signs
   of death, who was tracked down from plateaux
   but to ambush. Death is false light combined
   with shadow; black light is not the light among pines.

44
   Tragedy and myth are not bidden
   to broad Anogeia. The noon was full.
   The daughters of shot or burned bedridden
   people, were marched off and drawn by the pull
   of death's tidal lock about a spool.
   The cicadas kept making a racket.
   Evening an oven refusing to cool.
   The men and lads had taken their jackets
   from houses that burnt, as the moon stared in facets.

42 - SOE operatives held spectacular and notorious parties at their mansion 'Tara' on Gezira Island at Cairo. Patrick Leigh Fermor was 'Lord Rakehell', Xan Fielding was 'Lord Hughe Develdrive' and W. Stanley Moss was 'Mr Jack Jargon'. Medmanham abbey was Sir Francis Dashwood's infamous seat for the Hellfire Club in the 18th century. Fielding was Perkins' senior officer.
44 - The razing of Anogeia began on 13 August 1944 on the orders of General Müller and only ended on 5 September. The full moon was on 2 September, the last quarter on 11 August. The men were apprised of the approach of 2000 troops by sentries posted in other villages. Women and children were marched 19 km away. Every building in Anogeia was destroyed.

45

    The valley to the palace of Phaistos
    can be made out by light that is dark.
    Amari is the plain below Mt Kedros.
    The palace is the steps courtyard carpark
    by it now, where Idomeneus marked
    his son to die, as Müller did that place.
    He moved on *andartes* and oligarchs,
    to avenge the Kreipe kidnap disgrace –
    so he said. In reality to prevent a race,

46

    a hunt and steeplechase to Souda Bay,
    as the labyrinth collapsed, and troops
    withdrew from Heraklion. To delay
    the partisans' pursuit and regroup
    his forces, Müller attempted to dupe
    the Greeks by making Kreipe the excuse.
    Scorched earth was how he thought to recoup
    his garrison's position. Cruses
    went out round the unmazed palace, the more abstruse

45 – Phaistos Palace is a Minoan palace that dominated the Kedros Valley. The Cretan hero at Troy, Idomeneus, is actually recorded in the palace archives. He had sacrificed his own son (literally).

46 – Cruses? We are not to imagine electric lighting in these villages. Paraffin lamps if there was oil, but cruses just as when Phaistos Palace existed 1700–1200 BCE.

47
   of the Minoan complexes – for good.
   Zeus' cradle runs from Rethymno
   to Messara, where people have stood,
   and watched the phases of mountains flow
   past like moons along the fault lines' tow
   for ages now. Amari holds the rear
   to the two main coastal cities. Night glowed
   and smoke rose for a week – no one went near –
   wrote Psychoundrakis – the hamlets which disappeared.

48
   The communists then regained control
   of Kedros, they took the garrison
   at Scholi Asomaton, patrolled
   the passes and ambushed relief summoned
   from Rethymno. On the ridge, seasoned
   fighters disposed of the remainder.
   The Germans at Potami jettisoned
   the valley on 11 September,
   leaving the houses and fields and flesh in embers.

49
   When the battle of Potami was won,
   the partisans came down to liberate
   Heraklion. The triumphant one
   was Petrakis, who rode in some state
   through a joyous town. The Germans waited
   for the end of the war in Souda Bay –
   Müller flying to seal East Prussia's fate.
   Chania's residents felt betrayed,
   while Anglo-German condominium held sway.

50

Germany, where has your Athens gone?
Is it Delphi you want? Manichaean
foe of life and genius, you gave song
nonetheless, and mind Apollonian.
Now you fall back like the Athenians
at Syracuse, cruel Athens from Melos.
Crete stands in the Mediterranean.
Salamis greens, but not for your Belos.
The mountain throne empty, where he watched on jealous.

51

Oud' d'ét'estin ha tálaina Troià.
Germany and Greece are free of myth.
Warfighters were replaced by lawyers
and economists. Centaurs and lapiths
did never fight nor men with hippogryphs.
Germany again became powerful,
as the two Germanies rebuilt forthwith
then reunified. Scarce avowable
such power, though scale made it inevitable.

50 – Hölderlin's *Der Archipelagus* summed up and responded to in one stanza. I refer also to the Melian dialogue in Thucydides V whereby the Athenians justified their killing of all Melian males, and the destruction of the Athenian army on Sicily in Book VII.
51 & **53** the Greek is from the conclusion of Euripides' *Trojan Women* – 'wretched Troy no longer exists,' and 'it will overwhelm the city' (l. 1368).

52

Ancient Greece was too big to be ignored,
too small to cast power, until wresting
nations from Iran, it turned Minotaur
and cuckoo, once inside the Simurgh's nest
of Persia – where paradise died and rests
beneath sulphur basilisks and bismuth.
Kant is right – the ethical state is best.
Alexander was the toxic youth
of Führers. The Greece that survived him is the truth.

53

Epiklúsei pólin. The mountain
of small nations should be considering
how to prevent that. Start with the fountain
of small nations, Greece. A shivering
flame takes off from the bodies, withering
remorse. There are never enough tanks
to go round. Apart from hindering
harm, Germany should be leading the ranks
of nations, for a commonwealth of peace and thanks.

54

For this the black light beyond tragic
of Greece should suffice. Wisdom hatches
from the myth of the egg. By no magic
or gnosis, the hungry beak snatches
at truths, and creates systems in patches
and plastic modelling according to need.
Where Hellas' nest was woven and thatched,
the thrush never learns and safely feeds
on the Minotaur's worm. It goes free, for time breeds.

55

The poem is the discarded egg.
The Greeks' sacred office is to bury
the dead. Minos and Rhadamanthus peg
out the German war graves – not as furies,
but as civil servants in a hurry.
Psychoundrakis and Paterakis tend
the remains of General Bräuer – ferried
across, shot with Müller, who had this end
in mind: of burial on Crete amongst his men.

55 – I am not entering into the controversy of whether General Bruno Bräuer (1893–1947) committed war crimes or not, or whether Müller was the sole culprit. Both men were tried by a Greek court and executed by firing squad. But from 'The Iliad' onwards, from the return of Hector's body, it has been an index of civilisation to respect the remains of the dead. Greeks have particularly witnessed to this. George Psychoundrakis and Manolis Paterakis previously mentioned in Canto IV were indeed the cemetery caretakers who received Bräuer's remains in 1970.

Canto V

1

New Zealand knew Spenserian stanzas
before: its premier Alfred Domett
was Governor Grey's Sancho Panza.
Both worked to reduce Māori to subject
status, which meant repression directed
on the Waikato, and taxidermy
by means of an ethnographic project
on an indigenous enemy,
   through books, cantos, alexandrines and allegory.

1 - Alfred Domett's Spenserian and Schopenhauerian epic of New Zealand race relations and ethnography is 'Ranolf and Amohia' (1872). Domett (1811–87) was premier of New Zealand (August 1862-October 1863) under Governor Sir George Grey. It promoted the supersession of the Māori nation by settlers and its assimilation into the colonial population.

2

Domett wrote 'Ranolf and Amohia'
while Ngāti Mahuta were expelled
from Auckland, to catch pneumonia
in the July rains, without dwellings
shelter or fire as the torrents fell
near what is now mock-Tudor Drury.
Arthur Schopenhauer and Spenser's spell
failed to make exhibits of Māori.
They only preserved imperial poetry.

3

Recommended by Sir Harry Parkes
for the Crown Princess Frederick to read,
the New South Wales premier remarked
that Domett's work was an interesting screed
on how natives were superseded.
Her arts advisor was Jules Laforgue,
a Uruguayan who used to proceed
on lunar walks out to Charlottenburg,
as poetry was displayed in a Berlin morgue.

---

2 - Drury south of Auckland has a Tudor shopping centre.

3 - Sir Henry Parkes the premier of New South Wales (1872-75, 1877, 1878-83, 1887-89, 1889-91) suggested Domett's *Ranolf and Amohia* as reading to Kronprinzessin Victoria (1840-1901) the consort of the future Kaiser Friedrich III. Known in English as the Crown Princess Frederick or Empress Frederick, she had wanted to learn about Māori. Her French 'reader' and general cultural adviser was indeed the Franco-Uruguayan poet Jules Laforgue (1860-87) who served her 1881-86, and published *L'imitation de Notre Dame La Lune* in 1885.

CANTO V

4

Māori were Charrúa for all he cared.
The Pierrots ponced in the Fragonard bush,
as he did his best not to be scared
by the moon's light of mercury ambush.
Say, is there going to be a putsch?
Amohia is dragged up by Ranolf
to the colonial moon, calabash
and all, while settlers try to engulf
or kill off natives – folk precursors to Adolf.

5

What is Palmerston North? Hardly Berlin.
Between the Tararua Ranges
and Ruahines a river hairpins –
the Manawatū. The town is arranged
art deco on the flat, and is strangely
absent – just like de Chirico's plazas.
Monumental so young, it does not change –
while nigh underground the river passes.
There the Māori Battalion met, just as Mars

4 – Alfred Graf von Waldersee was contemplating a putsch, or coup, against Friedrich III and his consort, even before their accession. I have assimilated Domett's lovers Ranolf and Amohia to the Rona and the Moon aetiological legend of Māori. Charrúa were the indigenous people of Uruguay who were exterminated as a nation.

CRETE 1941

6

overtook Saturn in the evening
above the show grounds, and Venus coupled
with Jupiter – Mercury leavening
the dawn. A Company doubled
up over the gum, B Company, supple
in water, fishing for pennies,
C Company the cowboys, D troubled
with walkabout. Ngā Kamupene,
Northland's Ngā Kiri Kapia, Bay of Plenty's

7

Ngā Ruku Kapa, the East Coast's kaupoi,
Waikato to Ngāti walkabout,
assembled from the teal and turquoise
land. Mt Arete in women's surtout
to the east, solid Mt Hector which flouts
the cloud further south, were strange presages
in the Tararuas, of how devout
pakeha had been to Greece; how pages
of antique scholarship could be so contagious.

8

The people Sir Apirana Ngāta
summoned, deemed to be dying at his birth
in 1874, soon started
to have more births than deaths, filling those berths
on the 'Aquitania' when the Firth
of Clyde was reached. Soon each of those soldiers
would pass through Knossos' œil de bœuf.
In no time the rifles on their shoulders
would have been put to use, in ways no man divulges.

9

George Dittmer was in command – or Georg
should one say. This pākehā from Hawke's Bay
mentored Māori officers in accord
with the New Zealand light infantry way
of fighting, also the zest for affray
the warrior desires. George Bertrand
his 2IC was a teacher who stayed
in Taranaki. Dittmer depended
on Ngāti Mutunga's man for all of war's ends.

10

Ngāti Mutunga of Urenui –
boastful name for a quiet estuary,
which has produced great leaders. The tui
is an aggressive bird, whose family
is the fruit tree it saves from robbery.
Its wise plumes withhold the source of nectar,
yet does so with boldness and raillery.
Plants that have this beneficent vector
find the hoarse and liquid songster their protector.

---

8 – The *salon de l'œil de bœuf* (Eye of the Bull, or Bull's Eye) was the antechamber to the Royal Bedchamber at Versailles.
10 – To be blunt, Urenui refers to the male member.

11

    Rev. Robert Maunsell observed
    that Māori poetics are invested
    with shade. He meant the half-night reserved
    to the New Zealand bush, where day congests
    the outward eye with light that impresses
    itself, and is not meant to be looked at.
    He referred to the hidden ingress
    and exits of speech as a habitat
    where epiphytes swap in silence a samizdat

12

    of connections only apparent
    to initiates. *Te reo* beats
    the stand-up mike for rendering latent
    extreme experience, and repeating
    awe and sorrow. Poe's Dupin could tell meets
    and moots with meaning from where leaps were made
    elliptically. There is no shade on Crete
    however. There, bodies were betrayed
    to the sun, until a little earth was traded.

---

11 – *Te reo Māori* is the Māori language. I am quoting unpublished words from Rev. Robert Maunsell (1810–94) cited by Governor Sir George Grey in his preface to *Ngā Mōteatea* (1853), an anthology of Māori poems.

13

    The maze of stones versus the labyrinth
    of vegetation yields a different
    language. One highlights, the other synths
    anything. Each of them shows reverence
    in its own way, one by severance
    and distinction, the other by joining
    from the start. In fact the reference
    common to them both is Ithaca's groin
    of olive, where the marriage bed was appointed.

14

    Each thalassocracy learns the sea
    has no heart, certainly not the island
    they sail from – all ledge and liberty.
    They fight over trading posts and pylons
    for an emporium or asylum,
    once they come home to port. But what was Greece
    to Māori? They met other men's sirens,
    chimaeras and gods as they reinforced
    the Olympus front, guarding the long gorge courses.

---

13 – The marriage bed of Odysseus and Penelope in Odyssey XXIV.

15

> Perhaps John of Patmos is an answer.
> The nets of Britomart were cast wide,
> so that Greek remastered and advanced
> the Christian legicide by deicide.
> *Te Paipera Tapu* brought tidings
> of end times: of falling stars and wormwood
> and monsters out of the sea, confided
> to a lake of burning glass. Māori stood
> on the Aegean, that sea of apostlehood.

16

> 'What is the heart of fury?' the playwright
> Aeschylus asked. Māori had some idea
> of what drove Hitler. Against the fright
> of the man, they responded with a seer's
> matching rage that managed whatever fear
> they had, and mocked him for being nothing.
> The Furies accepted the law's arrears,
> but these men knew Hitler was not bluffing –
> practising hard on the bayonet bags' stuffing.

15 – *Te paipera tapu* is the 1868 edition of the Bible in Māori, translated from Hebrew, Aramaic and Greek by William Williams and Robert Maunsell.

19 – Field Marshal Wilhelm List (1880–1971) was in command of the Balkans operations of 1941. He was relieved of his command of Army Group South in Ukraine and southern Russia in November 1941 by Adolf Hitler and pensioned off. He did not send Hitler a congratulatory telegram on surviving the 20 July coup attempt in 1944. He was convicted of war crimes at Nuremberg against Serbian hostages and sentenced to life imprisonment, to be released on health grounds in 1952. A contempt for National Socialists is apparent in his regard, his demeanour and disposition.

17
    They knew him to be unappeasable
in his wrath, unlike themselves who saw
in him a beast quite defeasible,
when discerned through prophecy. Ngata tore
through the peace and light to reach the core
of realpolitik in the address
and reply debate. He put on record
Augustine of Hippo's emphasis
on violence, that consummates an empire's congress.

18
    General Papagos assigned the east coast
to British and Commonwealth divisions,
while he and the Yugoslavs engrossed
Italy's attention. A schism
opened between these fronts – abysm
widening as Field Marshal Wilhelm List
outflanked through the centre. Bombing missions
supported the Panzers' seaward thrusts,
while Gebirgsjäger infiltrated snow and mist.

19
    List was a man whom conscience got, yet truth
missed. No one that tall looked more uncertain
and indignant. He held himself aloof
in the plight of the residual Christian,
carrying out policies he questioned.
Doubts were not enough. Far too competent
for his good, he served 'life' – short version.
The self-made Bavarian Protestant
suffered from discontent, that was itself dissent.

20

    The Battalion had to defend
    Mt. Olympus in bad April weather.
    Holding the head of a pass, their line bent
    in a salient, where they endeavoured
    through high winds and heavy rain, while never
    losing contact with the enemy.
    Their first battle proved hard to sever
    themselves from. Pig runs had been seminaries
    for such conditions, giving them immunity,

21

    and teaching them to be invisible,
    inside downpours that blew horizontal
    against the slopes. How divisible
    a man is – his form sliced by torrential
    rain, and then cut up after frontal
    assault on Dannert wire. The surprise
    was that diggers showed as much potential
    as Gebirgsjäger themselves, when the skies
    turned the terrain and positions into surmise.

22

    Except the Germans were found jumping rock
    to rock and trampling the wire. 'Frightened? Run!'
    they called out in English – as if a flock
    needed shedding or singling for fun.
    A Bren gun and a foothold were won –
    fog was a mountain that opened and closed.
    Then the sons of the mist saw what the sons
    of rain can do. Into the steady flows
    the Battalion withdrew – hard water their roads

CANTO V

23

on a five hour march through the deluge.
Blood had been another rain – absolved
in the solid air. There was no refuge
in Thessaly – just the Axis involved
in getting to Athens. Units dissolved
before Thermopylae, where a holding
action to help the retreat was resolved
upon, even as the fronts folded;
but no such last stand as Herodotus once told.

24

Barrowclough took on Ferdinand Schörner
and not Xerxes, defending Tempe Pass.
Māori were put on the back burner
while the lawyer brigadier fought a mask
of Hitler. Schörner was Nazi top brass,
a superb if brutal organiser –
more corporate warrior than son of Mars.
On hairpin curves, he lost 15 Panzers.
Leonidas had been a good temporiser.

22 – Sheep dog trials are a pastoral farming sports event in many Anglosphere nations. They have been held in New Zealand near to where they began at Lake Wānaka since 1867.

25

    The Battalion dug into a marsh
    that had not been there when Leonidas
    fought. Orders were suddenly to march
    into Athens, and be in readiness
    to embark for Crete and build a fortress,
    if they could: start up Talos the robot,
    and make the island into a fastness.
    What Crete had been – none of them knew a jot.
    Strangeness did not stop the men from giving a lot.

26

    In Greece their fighting role veered between
    building trenchworks and defensive action.
    Pioneers in the great war, they were keen
    to fight without being distracted
    with digging all the time. The reaction
    of the enemy at Mt. Olympus,
    made them want to engage and gain traction
    on him. Digging-in led to an impasse –
    what they wanted was a feeling of impetus.

27

    It remains a mystery what Māori
    and the Germans learned about the other
    on Olympus, in overpowering
    rain, and the gale in which shouts were smothered.
    On disengaging, each side recovered
    itself as a fighting force, and renewed
    its purpose. What it was that hovered
    when the weather cleared, each side fully knew;
    revealed to one another when most out of view.

28

    As birds are to space, so are we to time.
At home in the open and not one place,
birds make their flights, while we flit sublime
migrating the ages at a pace
their wings of a season will never chase
up to. On the wing we breed nation states
and languages. Crete then was a base
where distant peoples determined its fate.
Birds that do not know their nests, still recall their mates.

29

    On the wing we die. We learn to outflank
spatial problems through time, yet that true home
of ours refuses us. Just as swifts shrank
to nothing to fill the sky, learned to comb
the air for water, sleep up in the dome
nonetheless denied them, despite the loft
of their lives – so we find ourselves homing
in on death, that the blue is not soft
but at last hard – time no longer to our profit.

30

    Der Oberkommando der Luftwaffe
and not Field Marshal List, had designed
Unternehmen Merkur. Crete offered
air power in the eastern Med, defined
by a radius from Egypt, winding
round to Syria and the Balkans.
To Student and Löhr, Crete was assigned
the mission of countering Malta –
the Sea of Libya soon to become a cauldron.

31

The disaster that broke in broad daylight
was Hermann-Bernhard Ramcke, a war-dog
rabid with race-hatred. Through the bright
air he comes down in his paratroop togs,
invisible as a wasp – the prologue
to years of slander. He casts no shadow.
His media would be twitter and blog,
if he lived these days. He made truth a widow
but the mountain he lands on, he stocks with ammo

32

glider-fed above the Maleme plain
against the Battalion. Crete secured
the southern flank of *Generalplan
Ost* and *Barbarossa*, for rest-cure
colonies and planted people – immured
in farmland and settled as fencibles.
In a month that kind of empire recurs –
the sight of Pākehā insensible
to Pākehā, behaving indefensibly.

31 – The first line from the edition of *Ngā Mōteatea* by Sir Apirana Ngata: *i te puta tū ata i whakarakea i te awatea.*

32 – To many colonised nations and peoples all over the world, the second world war in Europe presented the spectacle of colonial powers acting towards themselves as they had done towards indigenes and subject nations and peoples. *Pākehā* is the Māori word for a European person. Fencibles were the military settlers on plots of land around the early settler towns in New Zealand.

CANTO V

33

The gauze fly and the desert fox will row.
Here's my America. The wasp attacks
Trent Park, the London Cage, even chow
time at Camp Clinton with his buzz – snatches
of peace only come when he dispatches
himself from talk of knights, robbers and ghosts.
A Christmas manhunt along the Natchez
trace for the state of Mississippi's most
wanted Nazi and wannabe radio host.

34

We have each gone down the Führer-hole.
The 28th Battalion did so
with a bayonet charge, for which the goal
was a swastika flag. Their arms borne low
they heaved their breath – Ah Ah Ah – in one go,
broke into a run, made for German fire,
while D Company struck as one blow
and cleared the field at Maleme. Inspired
to do this – since that was what the job required.

---

33 – I refer to facilities in the UK and USA where German generals were imprisoned. Ramcke did escape for all of four days from Camp Clinton, Mississippi, from 1 January 1946. He was recaptured by Epiphany. I refer to William Faulkner's *Light in August* and to the character Joe Christmas, and to Goethe's reflections on America in *Wilhelm Meisters Lehrjahre* and his poem 'Amerika – du hast es besser', and I refer to T.S. Eliot's 'Journey of the Magi'. Truly – *'Hier, oder nirgend ist Amerika!'*.
34 – An action on 22 May 1941.

35

So much for coloured fugitivity.
Even Major Dyer, who witnessed
the attack, and thought a proclivity
to take defeat easily, diminished
Māori in assault, was astonished
at seeing the men's true combat style
revived. 33 fell in that skirmish
which carried the field – full frontal, no guile –
nothing like an enfilade coming up in file.

36

The Battalion then retired to where
they started from – Platanias – its hills
old cliffs from the former coast. With care
General Ringel worked forward, instilled
with Austrian mountain skills, to fill
space around a position, so it fell
from withdrawal – topped by overspill.
Any successes at repelling
Gebirgsjäger, was offset by their rationale

37

to be like those kri-kri on the island
off Platanias, the 28th's
starting point. On that coast, guns were silenced
after the Battle of Pink Hill. Too late
to try and win back the plain from the weight
of pounding aircraft, infantry numbers.
The wild goats stayed to populate
the island and Crete, having been plundered
on the mainland for the partisans' provender.

38
　The goats stayed and the Battalion left.
　Kopfhautjäger – what's that supposed to mean?
　It means *taiaha*. The whole land is cleft
　at the Awatere Valley, unseamed.
　Only theogony could be the theme
　of such a place, until the impact
　and the river's fast long wound hurt one keen.
　The poem is a web that keeps intact
　in the wind: it flutters, its bit of skin distracts.

39
　The mountain is more than a land's woe.
　It is where all legends end their voyage.
　A grave of Zeus. The Old Man. And his throes
　have finished. Stillness is what is salvaged
　from the debris on the trail and rampage
　inland. Eponymous river and flats:
　nothing like Lethe has haemorrhaged
　along your banks, but our poor surrogate
　amnesia eddies, while memory is rued down pat.

37 – The *kri-kri* – the Cretan wild goats were introduced to a sanctuary on the island offshore from Platanias in 1936. Those recent arrivals survived those events.

38 – *Kopfhautjäger* = scalphunters. A *taiaha* is a Māori weapon of war resembling a spear, which is the instrument of a martial art. The Awatere Valley is a magnificent place in the East Cape of the North Island in New Zealand. The land assumes another scale there. The sacred mountain Hikurangi stands over it all; the Awatere river flows NNE.

40

Arapeta Awatere sings
waiata for the Battalion
for the men it lost. He had been all things
in time: Theseus and Asterion.
His Greek and Latin un-Palladian
un-Parnassian, he knew the wood
of Britomart's carving, the Daedalan
art of Crete. For him a poem was good
if it had been appeased – wept as much as it could.

41

The woman is necessary, who gives
shape to the night and makes something else
happen than darkness. Nothing starts to live
or otherwise without her, even pulse
already beating. Without her, a *danse
macabre* takes him off and spins him round.
Without her body overnight, he quells
no obduracy in nature – is found
guilty of failure for good on love's wounded ground.

---

40 – Lieut. Colonel Arapeta Awatere (1910–76) was Commanding Officer of the 28th (Māori) Battalion in an acting capacity in 1944, and then appointed Commander Officer. He led the Battalion to victory over 1944-45. Of Ngāti Hine and Ngāti Porou affiliations, he was a profound scholar of Greek and Latin verse (which he quoted in the original), and of English verse. He also composed Māori *waiata* – laments and songs. He was a profound student of war history, and dedicated his classical scholarship to that purpose as well. Convicted of murder in 1965, he died in prison just before his parole.

42
    Victory is a diorama
    set ablaze. Think how they descended
    one bank of the River Gaiana
    as infantry, and reascended
    as marines in the airquake crescendo
    of a creeping barrage while a bask
    of crocodiles torches innuendos
    of gunfire. Culmination of the task
    of those years – damage done to one, no one need ask.

43
    Colonel Eruera Love would not use
    exploding bullets. Forward positions
    were risky for all – in his case losing
    his life to an airburst, was admission
    the just suffered too. Soldiers' vision
    at the foot of the cross will be baffled,
    not knowing what they say in conditions
    transfigured. Shouts Awatere – rattled:
    'Get up Padre! Don't crawl!' in prayer before battle.

44
    The country is a crayfish broken
    open. Race is a cracked carapace,
    because the enemy had woken
    an ethnic apocalypse, which we faced
    up to. Then we dined on it with bad grace,
    and threw the leftovers to the seagulls.
    Battalion veterans worked to erase
    Kiwi racism, having helped annul
    the worst racial programme of killing and culling.

45

    Star axes, the *astropeléki*,
    are lightning bolts and the meteor.
    Such flashes have no entelechy;
    they are butts from the mind's humidor,
    really bad for our health. The matadors
    must have done a good job vaulting the bulls.
    Minos hammed it as Commendatore
    to Don Giovanni, but still just as cruel.
    Watch the octopus grab the crayfish in the pool.

46

    Ants are guarding their underworld tunnel.
    Cataglyphis creticus loves dust roads,
    such as those New Zealanders funnelled
    down to Sfakia. It carried loads
    of our last rations to its deepest nodes.
    Temnothorax minotaurosis
    adapted to a dry abode,
    creeps in and out of the dust's jalousies,
    slim-waist like geometric ware symposia.

47

    Melissa tends thyme and sage bee gardens
    on Crete, domesticates the one fly
    that can use agave or cardamon
    alike. Could their buzz hide a babe's cry?
    Zeus is a drone that pollinates the sky.
    Expect the tomb of Zeus to be a hive
    a Mycenaean *tholos*. Here Zeus died,
    pulled in from the cold, while still alive.
    Not Minos euhemeristically deified.

48

These are the native *pōpokorua*
of New Zealand, the endemic ants
of our isles: stinging *Pachycondyla
castanea* – the brown bush ant extant
in all our forests and the occupants
of insect Tartarus, *Heberia
striata*, which drag snails down to claimant
mouths alive. Their shells are scoria,
discarded inside the ant nest's aporia.

49

Melissa's bees are pushing out our own.
A case of colonisation from Crete
in apiculture – not just the old clones
of state. The manuka honey rush beats
endemic bees to the draw. Their seat
a single hole, *Leioproctus fulvescens*
ensures a lone larva is replete
and fed like a god – pollen excrescent
not out of leg-bags but carried obsolescent

50

in the stomach. Of the little diggers,
lasioglossum sordidus likes dirt
from ditches and stop-banks. It figures
that it likes herbicide-cleared ground. The hurt
soil would have created ideal desert
for a utopian solitude.
It takes such stingless bees to insert
their singular settlement and brood –
a *locus amoenus* amidst the turpitude.

51

    Still, dig into ants or honey bees' nests
    out in the wild, and we will discover
    the *hāngi* the insects have invested
    for themselves. Knossos – which was another
    such comb – is the poor and empty mother
    of government, a stone *umu* agape.
    Some things are best left covered. We hover
    wondering at the overall shape.
    A government dies and we dispense with the crêpe.

52

    Death is a small hole or else corporal.
    The air's stillness is a matter of poise
    as the cicadas thresh the chaparral –
    louder than beating blood or the heart's noise
    on the run. They do this without voices.
    The mouth without sound is articulate
    for descent. No seraph consoled the boys
    in cawls of flame or for hot scrap that hit
    their fright of flesh – there is only mouth and no pit

53

    except for the one of Knossos, which keeps
    reiterating. I – a small voice come
    from Blenheim – say these lines, before I leap
    into dust myself. States are not the sum
    of things, nor have these poems the wisdom
    to manage either. Plato's synod
    is over; the three wayfarers are numb
    from all their talking, for whom the tripod
    came apart, of Crete, Athens, Sparta – *Ichabod*.

54
    Strange how the eagle and wren once fought
    over Crete, and now enter new mazes
    of power together. 80 years brought
    us a new scale. Versailles went to blazes –
    Westphalia is an historic phase.
    We learn to bury. That two small nations
    once fought a giant eagle, amazes
    even now. Greece and New Zealand's stations
    have not changed: power is now a new creation.

55
    Crete is the island. Once Germany
    New Zealand and Greece and the Austrians
    were in conflict for supremacy
    on the isle. Only the Cretans won.
    Do not look for ruins of Minoans
    but go on a search for the grave of Zeus –
    see where the flowers have dominion.
    Poetry was the monster. Hold the truce,
    but pick none of the flowers where death ran so loose.

CRETE 1941

Sonnet to Hölderlin

Germany has places where time stands
in pools alive, even though these pools
are dry and are still expecting hands
to use them, if only to feel how cool
in the shade or warm in the sun stone is.
As if the fountain needed hands far more
than it needs water. For now the practice
is fire that makes us new stars, and stores
up in our minds all the water wept
in the world. Even as circumcision
and the old baptism intercept
with our passion's fury and fission
to be dispensed with, so pours desire
through cut threefold basins. And time is fire.

Oxford
18 January 2019

The great German poet Friedrich Hölderlin (1770–1843) studied at the Lutheran School at Maulbronn, Württemberg, the Evangelisches Seminar Kloster Maulbronn, which had been a Cistercian monastery. A marvellous lavatorium or wash fountain stands outside the refectory. The school counts Johannes Kepler, Friedrich Hölderlin, Eduard Mörike and Hermann Hesse amongst its alumni. The theologian David Friedrich Strauss taught there.

Hölderlin took Romantic verse to its farthest frontier. He had suffered a complete mental breakdown by 1806 and was kept in a tower along the Neckar river until his death, having lost his identity.

Coda

A catalogue of donors is required
to thank those who brought this work to print
to acknowledge those who were prior
those who gave the poem unstinting
support and those who made themselves present
some way. To them this is a testament
that runs across generations
uniting nations in commemoration.

Chaucer began with a knight. I will start
with a New Zealand prime minister.
It took Sir William English to part
us from Alfred Domett's filibuster
of verse. The best strategist Westminster
government had in our generation.
Such premiers have made the sinister
art of the past face a new creation
in policy – partnership not relegation.

Next Mr Speaker Trevor Mallard
who wrote the gracious foreword to this piece –
a power in the Labour Cabinet forwards.
Wise and judicious, you honour the fleece.
Just as you order the House, you brought peace
to race relations. Sir Michael Cullen
passed before this poem could be released.

To a politics notably sullen
towards intellect, he brought stringent acumen.

Then there is Treasury, and Bill Moran
in whom governance found its architect.
Did I live before our friendship began?
It preceded everyone else's checks
and balances – one of the good effects
of Viard College. Treasury is proof
of the New Zealand mind. Thank you Becky
and Tim – Mr Governor Gabs Makhlouf
for that Pharos' relentless light of truth.

Vangelis – MFAT's astute logothete
warrants deep thanks for his warm interest
while the poem was being completed.
His generosity found confluence
with Australia's philanthropists
from Crete – kind Tony Tsourdalakis.
Olympia Bobou influenced
how this work of many Greeces – focused
on corrections – acted as its own archivist.

America too has shared its cargo
of literature and munificence.
Mr Carroll Joynes of Chicago
nobly recognised significance
in a project that is a romance
and tragedy of Crete. The Cato
Trust in Waikato improved the chance
of the poem coming out in octavo.
Epic that might not have been condemned by Plato.

Adrian and Seamus Kennedy
and I had Dunedin's Robbie Burns
for a clubrooms where we sought remedies
for the state of poetry. Now in turn
we make our contribution – discerning
the need for New Zealanders to recognise
Realpolitik's dangers – and also learn
from how states have fallen and capsized.
With those two brothers this epic was exercised.

Can a civilisation as ancient
and deep as China be expressed in one man?
Yes – if the man is ethical – patient
and good as Dr Chin – whose virtue spans
four thousand years. Friendship is its own plan.
Note Ramsey and Despina Margolis –
Girol Karacaoglu who began
Co-op Bank – then far from holus bolus –
Richard Cross listening to an Aïda chorus.

Germany and Austria have patrons
too – Malte Nuhn – Norman Franke
and Hanno Scheuch. The citron
blooms on Crete as well. I extend warm thanks
for your interest in paratactic flanks
by air sea and mountain. In this story –
Gebirgsjäger – paratroopers – not tanks
or ordnance prevailed. As for glory –
that is left to Cretans who endured this history.

Thanks to the godfather of this poem
Sir Wira Gardiner without whom these words
would never have been written. At his home

at Te Kaha this writing first occurred
when the Ngārimu sonnet unfurled
in the mind. My lively gratitude
to Tania Simpson who proffered
such endorsement – to Trevor Moeke's prelude
that compels living and the dead to similitude.

Son of the desert – wise Lord of War
you made this epic necessary
from our encounters in the bookstore.
Nations do not have a cemetery
for then they would be complementary.
I am a local time with the hourglass
broken. Genius of the dunes – theory
we know – arises from how we surpass
experience. This epic is a time recast.

Support for the crowdfunding campaign from Tony Tsourdalakis was on behalf of the Cretan Federation of Australia & New Zealand.

About the author

Born in New Zealand in 1961, Bernard Cadogan is an accomplished poet, philosopher and historian. Since 1996, he has worked as a political advisor and speech writer, in particular as policy advisor to the prime minister. He has been a consultant to the New Zealand Treasury since 2011 and was appointed an honorary advisor to the Māori king in 2015.

He is especially interested in the philosophy of Paul Ricoeur, John Rawls and Charles Taylor, and his current focus is on postcolonial thought, the formation of empires, and the resilience, relevance and viability of small nation states.

Bernard holds a DPhil from Oxford University on the political thought, constitutionalism and racial policy of Sir George Grey (1812–98) in Australia, New Zealand and South Africa. He lives in the Cherwell Valley, near Oxford, with his wife Jacqueline and their three children.

Thanks

Many good friends responded to this poem as it was being written, helped and advised in various ways. Some influenced me as a poet or in my knowledge of how nation states think and behave. I would like to begin by acknowledging my immense debt to a New Zealand poet, the late Hone Tuwhare (1922–2008) and to express my gratitude for his witness to poetry, from when I first met him in 1978. I also wish to acknowledge a distinguished poet in Arabic, the Palestinian poet Walid Khazendar who has given me such wise counsel here at Oxford.

I wish to give especial thanks and express deep gratitude to Trevor Moeke for the magnificent karakia he composed for 'Crete 1941'. I wish also to acknowledge with corresponding gratitude the thoughtful and generous words of Rt Hon Trevor Mallard in his foreword. I thank Adrian Kennedy, Rt. Hon Sir William English KNZM, Sir Harawira Gardiner KNZM, Hon Sir Michael Cullen KNZM, Rt. Hon Simon Upton, Hon Hugh Templeton AO QSO, Gabriel Makhlouf, Bill Moran MNZM, Dr Hanno Scheuch, Hon Justin Shaw, Vangelis Vitalis, Dr Girol Karacaoglu, Dr Olympia Bobou, Dr Mark Hickford, and Carolyn Heath.

I would also like to acknowledge Dr Norman Franke, Professor Theo van Lint and Haig Utidjian, Professor Lydia Wevers, Professor Richard Hill, Dr Richard Reeve, Professor Peter Skegg, Professor Gordon Parsonson BEM, Dr Hugh Macmillan, AB Abrams, Su Cullen Wetere, Rongo Wetere ONZM, Dr Salvador Venegas-Andraca, Dr Dan Sperrin, Dr Warren Limbrick, Dr Eric Chin and Dian Schalk, Dr Tom McLean, Jonathan Hames, and Mathew Madain. My deepest gratitude goes to Ramsey Margolis and Winton Higgins of Tuwhiri for such a sensitive and carefully-produced edition of the poem. And of course I thank my wife Jacqueline for her tireless support.

Tuwhiri thanks

The following *Crete 1941 Sponsors* whose generous support through our PledgeMe campaign ensured the publication of this book.

Cato Trust
Eric Chin
Sir Bill English
Carroll Joynes
Adrian Kennedy
Trevor Mallard
Bill Moran
Tony Tsourdalakis,
    President, Cretan Federation of Australia & New Zealand
Vangelis Vitalis

TUWHIRI

A small group of people from Aotearoa New Zealand and Australia came together not so long ago to publish a book. Looking for a name for our imprint that would express what we stood for as secular Buddhist practitioners, we adopted a word in te reo Māori: Tuwhiri. This was our way of acknowledging and respecting the tangata whenua, the indigenous people of Aotearoa.

This idea was discussed within and beyond the small community of secular Buddhists in our two countries. 'Tuwhiri' captures our response to our encounter with the forms of Buddhism that had arrived in our countries. The notion of revealing, making known, discovering something lost or hidden, matched our experience of finding fresh insights in the early Buddhist teachings when we examine them anew.

Secular Buddhism is a trend in contemporary western Buddhism which highlights care – the fundamental ethic in the teachings of the historical Buddha – in all its aspects. Secularity calls on us to express this ethic of care in ways appropriate to our time and current predicaments.

In the face of humanity-induced catastrophes – not least the climate emergency and intensifying social injustices – we owe a special duty of care to future generations to overcome them, and to leave our successors with a safer, fairer world in which they may thrive. We need to express our care for coming generations in many ways, from changing our own personal lifestyles, through accounting for our history, to choosing political representatives who advance long-sighted policies in aid of a better world.

This book makes no claim to Buddhist inspiration. However, it serves to make all who read it even more aware of the wrongs perpetrated by those who colonised Aotearoa, and the need to settle the claims that have arisen from this process. Thus Tuwhiri takes pleasure in publishing it.

To find out about The Tuwhiri Project, please go to:

https://tuwhiri.nz/about

CPSIA information can be obtained
at www.ICGtesting.com
Printed in the USA
FSHW022023081121
85938FS